Access to History

Rivalry and Accord: International Relations 1870–1914

Access to History

General Editor: Keith Randell

Rivalry and Accord: International Relations 1870–1914

John Lowe

Hodder & Stoughton

A MEMBER OF THE HODDER HEADLINE GROUP

The cover illustration shows Kaiser Wilhelm II
(Courtesy Bildarchiv Preussicher Kulturbesitz, Berlin)

Order: Please contact Bookpoint Ltd, 39 Milton Park, Abingdon,
Oxon OX14 4TD. Telephone: (44) 01235 400414. Fax: (44) 01235 400454.
Lines are open from 9 am - 6 pm Monday to Saturday, with a 24-hour
message answering service. Email address: orders@bookpoint.co.uk

British Library Cataloguing in Publication Data

Lowe, John
  Rivalry and accord : international relations
  1870-1914.–(Access to
  History).
  1. Foreign relations, 1870-1914
  I.Title   II. Series
  327'.09'034

ISBN 0-340-51806 5

First published in Great Britain 1998 in Access to A-Level History series
Access to History edition first published 1990
Impression number   19 18 17 16 15 14 13 12
Year   2004 2003 2002 2001 2000

Typeset by Photo Graphics, Honiton, Devon.
Printed in Great Britain for Hodder & Stoughton Educational,
a division of Hodder Headline Plc, 338, Euston Road, London NW1 3BH
by Redwood Books, Trowbridge, Wiltshire.

Contents

Preface

To the general reader

Although the *Access to History* series has been designed with the needs of students studying the subject at higher examination levels very much in mind, it also has a great deal to offer the general reader. The main body of the text (i.e. ignoring the Study Guides at the ends of chapters) forms a readable and yet stimulating survey of a coherent topic as studied by historians. However, each author's aim has not merely been to provide a clear explanation of what happened in the past (to interest and inform): it has also been assumed that most readers wish to be stimulated into thinking further about the topic and to form opinions of their own about the significance of the events that are described and discussed (to be challenged). Thus, although no prior knowledge of the topic is expected on the reader's part, she or he is treated as an intelligent and thinking person throughout. The author tends to share ideas and possibilities with the reader, rather than passing on numbers of so-called 'historical truths'.

To the student reader

There are many ways in which the series can be used by students studying History at a higher level. It will, therefore, be worthwhile thinking about your own study strategy before you start your work on this book. Obviously, your strategy will vary depending on the aim you have in mind, and the time for study that is available to you.

If, for example, you want to acquire a general overview of the topic in the shortest possible time, the following approach will probably be the most effective:

1. Read chapter 1 and think about its contents.
2. Read the 'Making notes' section at the end of chapter 2 and decide whether it is necessary for you to read this chapter.
3. If it is, read the chapter, stopping at each heading or ⋆ to note down the main points that have been made.
4. Repeat stage 2 (and stage 3) where appropriate) for all the other chapters.

If, however, your aim is to gain a thorough grasp of the topic, taking however much time is necessary to do so, you may benefit from carrying out the same procedure with each chapter, as follows:

1. Read the chapter as fast as you can, and preferably at one sitting.
2. Study the flow diagram at the end of the chapter, ensuring that you understand the general 'shape' of what you have just read.
3. Read the 'Making notes' section (and the 'Answering essay

questions' section, if there is one) and decide what further work you need to do on the chapter. In particularly important sections of the book, this will involve reading the chapter a second time and stopping at each heading and * to think about (and to write a summary of) what you have just read.

4. Attempt the 'Source-based questions' section. It will sometimes be sufficient to think through your answers, but additional under-standing will often be gained by forcing yourself to write them down.

When you have finished the main chapters of the book, study the 'Further Reading' section and decide what additional reading (if any) you will do on the topic.

This book has been designed to help make your studies both enjoyable and successful. If you can think of ways in which this could have been done more effectively, please write to tell me. In the meantime, I hope that you will gain greatly from your study of History.

Keith Randell

CHAPTER 1

Introduction: Europe and the Great Powers

1 The Franco-Prussian War, 1870–71

In July 1870, the French government threw caution to the winds and blundered into a conflict with Prussia. By declaring war to avenge a slight to her national honour, the French fell into a trap that Bismarck, the Prussian king's chief minister, had carefully laid for them. War against France, the 'traditional enemy', was Bismarck's best chance of persuading the independent south German states to unite with the Prussian-dominated states of north Germany. Bismarck found an issue that could be exploited to provoke France when he secretly pressed the claims of a distant relative of the King of Prussia to the vacant Spanish throne. To Bismarck's dismay, however, the plot misfired and France scored a diplomatic victory by issuing a dignified and restrained protest against the 'Prussian' candidature. But the French government, pushed on by bellicose public opinion, foolishly demanded 'guarantees' from the King of Prussia that the claims of his relatives would never be renewed. In a remarkable display of ingenuity, Bismarck edited the king's factual report of his encounter with the French ambassador to read as a deliberate insult to France. When this version – 'a red rag to the Gallic bull' as Bismarck called it – was published in the press, France's honour could only be satisfied by a declaration of war.

The Franco-Prussian war was a disaster for France. She entered the war without allies and with a badly organised army. Its slow and inefficient mobilisation put her at an immediate disadvantage compared with the Prussian army whose mobility was remarkable. Although some French regiments fought heroically, the bulk of the army was no match for the well-trained, highly disciplined and well-led Prussians and their German allies. The French were not only outnumbered and outgunned. They were also completely outmanoeuvred.

The outcome was decided by two major encounters in the opening stages of the war. At Sedan, in early September, one French army was defeated and surrendered with over 80 000 men as well as the French Emperor. In late October, the main French army of over 150 000 men, which had been encircled for over two months at Metz, capitulated. The war continued for another three months as the Government of National Defence, which replaced the discredited Second Empire, raised new armies to fight the Prussians. Despite a few successes the new armies failed to break the siege of Paris, which had been cut off from the rest of France since mid-September. Paris finally fell in January 1871, after a terrible ordeal.

The peace terms were severe. The victors demanded the cession of Alsace and Lorraine, two provinces with rich iron ore deposits, textile industries and good agricultural land. An indemnity of 5000 million francs was demanded and until it was paid German troops occupied parts of France. A final humiliation was a victory march through Paris.

France's troubles were not over with the ending of the war. Paris, which had suffered severely during the long siege, set itself up as a rival authority to the government and the newly elected Assembly at Versailles. After the proclamation of a 'Commune', a socialist and workers' regime was inaugurated in late March 1871. When the Communards refused to agree to the government's terms, troops took the city by force in late May, amidst scenes of appalling ferocity.

* The Franco-Prussian war had enormous implications for Europe. The unification of Germany was facilitated by the participation of the south German states in a victorious war against France. The King of Prussia was proclaimed German Emperor in the Hall of Mirrors at the palace of Versailles in January 1871. The incorporation of the southern states, including Bavaria and Würtemberg (though not the 10 million Germans in Austria), into the new German Empire transformed the political situation in central Europe. Instead of a relatively weak collection of states with powerful neighbours on each side, 'Germany' was now a major power and growing in strength as her economy expanded, assisted by political unity.

The defeat of France marked the end of an era in which she had been regarded as the great military power on the continent, alongside Russia. The success of the Prussian military machine in 1870–71 necessitated a reappraisal of conventional military wisdom. It demonstrated the importance of a competent General Staff, capable of planning military operations and utilising railways effectively for the rapid movement of supplies and deployment of troops. Future wars, it was widely believed, would be wars of movement and of short duration, with a premium on rapid mobilisation. Conscription was also shown to be necessary to provide adequate trained reserves, while the Prussian education system was hailed as contributing to the superiority of her armies over semi-literate French peasant soldiers.

The emergence of a powerful German Empire upset the existing balance of power in Europe. Prussia's defeat of France in 1871 came hard on the heels of her defeat of Austria in 1866. This left Russia as the only other major military power on the continent and even her reputation had suffered a bad blow from her defeat by Britain and France in the Crimean War of 1854–56. But she was able to take advantage of the war in 1870 to denounce the restrictions which had been imposed on her maintaining a navy in the Black Sea. Italy also

See Preface for explanation of * symbol

gained from the war, occupying Rome in 1870, which had hitherto been denied her by the presence of French troops defending the interests of the papacy. The defeat of France in 1870–71, therefore, marked the culmination of a series of changes that created a new system of international relations in Europe, in which Germany was likely to play a dominant role.

2 Germany

From 1815 until the Austro-Prussian war of 1866, the term 'Germany' did not signify a great power, but a loose confederation of 39 states of very variable size. The two most powerful were Austria and Prussia, who were also great powers in their own right. Although Prussia did not begin to challenge Austria's political predominance in Germany until the 1850s, she had, by this time, established an economic ascendancy by means of a customs union (the *Zollverein*).

The German Empire, proclaimed in January 1871, was the product of 'blood and iron', as Bismarck expressed it. Since unification had been brought about through three wars fought by Prussia against Denmark, Austria and France, the new German state was in many important respects modelled on Prussia.

This was most evident in the authoritarian and militaristic nature of the German Empire. Executive power (decision making) belonged to the Kaiser (Emperor) and the Chancellor (chief minister), while other ministers acted as their agents. The Chancellor and the ministers were appointed by the Kaiser and were not answerable to parliament, as opposed to the British system. The Kaiser was also Supreme War Lord, which gave the military chiefs the right of direct access to him, bypassing the ministers.

This authoritarian political structure was given a democratic façade in the form of a *Reichstag* elected by universal suffrage, but it was unable to exercise much control over the government, except in budgetary matters. In practice, however, the Imperial Chancellor was anxious to have the co-operation of the *Reichstag* in passing laws and in order to make governing the newly created state easier. Strenuous efforts were therefore made to secure a pro-government majority from among the parties of the centre and right.

* From 1871 to 1890, Germany was dominated by Bismarck. The old Kaiser, William I, who was already 64 when he had become King of Prussia in 1861, trusted him on most issues and his prestige as the creator of a united Germany was enormous. Bismarck was also an extremely able politician and statesman. After 1890, a lack of co-ordination was evident in German diplomacy, partly because policy-making was shared amongst the new Kaiser (Wilhelm II), the Chancellor and the foreign minister, as well as the military and naval chiefs.

Between 1871 and 1914, Germany became the greatest industrial power in Europe. Unification, creating a single internal market, contributed to her rapid economic expansion, despite temporary recessions. German industrialisation was characterised by the growth of heavy industry (iron and steel) and the emergence of new industries (chemicals and optics), as well as by rapid urbanisation.

* Germany's rapid industrialisation was significant in several ways. By 1900, she had outstripped Britain, previously the leading industrial nation in Europe, and was second in the world only to the United States. The growth of the German economy intensified the competition amongst industrial states for markets and raw materials. This, combined with population growth, increased the pressure for overseas colonies. Within Germany, it generated considerable social tension. The growth of a large industrial working class and an expanding middle class should, perhaps, have resulted in a liberal-democratic regime. Instead, an authoritarian political structure contributed to the continued social dominance of the traditional land-owning Prussian aristocracy (*Junkers*). Some historians have argued that the German government sought to defuse social tension by using foreign policy as a diversionary tactic – success abroad was to distract attention away from internal problems. In the Bismarckian decades, it is said, colonial policy was to serve this purpose – hence the term 'social imperialism'. Under Wilhelm II, overseas policy in general (*Weltpolitik*) was used for the same ends.

Imperial Germany was likely to follow the traditions of Prussian foreign policy, especially under Bismarck's guidance. This implied co-operation with the other conservative powers, Austria-Hungary and Russia. Relations with Russia were reinforced by dynastic links with the Tsars and underpinned, at least for a decade, by economic ties (the exchange of German manufactures for Russian grain) until conflicts over tariffs began. A possible alternative orientation to German foreign policy was on the lines of friendship between the 'Anglo-Saxon' nations, a revival of the old alliance of Protestant powers. There was also a dynastic link between the Prussian royal family and Victorian Britain. This raised a fundamental question that was never properly answered: should Germany regard herself as Britain's partner or rival in world trade and empire?

3 France

French power in Europe was at its height under Napoleon, when France was still the wealthiest and, barring Russia, the most populous nation on the continent. For many years after his defeat in 1815, France continued to be regarded as a threat to the peace of Europe.

This was only partly due to her reputation as a military nation. She was also feared as the home of revolutionary ideas, a view that was reinforced when revolutions broke out in France in 1830 and again in 1848, spreading to other parts of Europe.

In terms of international relations, however, these fears were not really justified. From 1815 to 1852 France pursued a largely pacific foreign policy, sometimes co-operating with Britain in a sort of 'liberal alliance'. The real challenge to the existing European order came with the reign of Napoleon III (nephew of the great Napoleon) from 1852 to 1870. During this period, Russia was defeated by France and Britain acting in alliance – the 'Crimean Coalition' of 1854. French armies also fought in north Italy in 1859 in the 'war of liberation', directed against Austria – a sign of Napoleon's sympathy for the cause of 'nationality'. For the same reason, France stayed neutral when Prussia fought Austria in 1866, enabling Prussia to unite the north German states under her leadership. In 1870–71, France paid the price for Napoleon's miscalculation in fostering the growth of Prussian power.

France made a rapid recovery from her defeat in the early 1870s and regained her status as a great power. Her reorganised army, now based on universal service, came to be regarded as an effective military force. She also developed a powerful navy although it suffered, at times, from having too many prototypes and not being a homogeneous fleet.

The Franco-Prussian war was fought as a war between equals, in demographic and economic terms. By 1914, however, there was a marked disparity between the two states in both population and industrial strength. France's industrialisation was slower, more spasmodic and less complete than Germany's. This showed most obviously in output of coal, iron and steel but also in the high proportion of her population still engaged in farming. The French rate of population increase was much less than Germany's and lower than that of all the other great powers. Nevertheless, France remained a very wealthy country. Vast amounts of capital were invested abroad, especially in Russia – three times as much as was invested in her overseas empire.

Politically, the contrast between France and Germany was also quite striking. The 1875 Constitution made France into a democratic republic with extensive individual liberties. In contrast to both Germany and Britain, executive power was weak. One result was that short-lived governments had difficulty in keeping control over enthusiasts for imperial expansion, whether they were officials in the Colonial Office or ambitious officers in the colonial army. Another was that frequent changes of government did not make for consistency in policies although, sometimes, a minister retained his post through several such changes.

The influence of the idea of *revanche* (revenge) for the defeat of 1871 on the policies of French governments can easily be exaggerated. Nevertheless, it persisted as an ideal – something that should not be forgotten – for many Frenchmen. Most Republicans, however, were preoccupied with consolidating the new regime on a durable basis against the threats (real or imagined) from Catholic monarchists and aristocratic army officers. What emerged was a conservative republic attentive, for the most part, to the interests of the bourgeoisie and peasantry. By 1900, the French Left (Socialists and Radicals) was largely pacifist and anti-militarist in outlook. On the other hand, a vocal section of the French Right had become very nationalistic and committed to *revanche*. The fact that France had a republican regime did not, of itself, preclude good relations with monarchical states. The tarnished image of the Third Republic, however, resulting from corruption and scandals, did play a part in deterring the Tsar from signing an alliance with France before the mid-1890s.

   * In the 1870s, French foreign policy reverted to the tradition of the liberal alliance with Britain. In the following decade, however, colonial rivalries soured Anglo-French relations, especially in Africa. France herself became a great imperial power in this period with extensive colonial possessions in Africa and Asia. The alliance with Russia, signed in 1892–94, became the keystone of French foreign policy and her guarantee of security against an increasingly powerful Germany. In practice, however, the alliance seemed to be anti-British in its direction until 1904, when France reached a colonial agreement with Britain. The entente of 1904 began as not much more than an indication of an amicable relationship, but demonstrations of German hostility towards France between 1905 and 1911 gradually converted it, by 1914, into something approaching a military alliance between France and Britain.

4 Great Britain

Britain was one of the leading great powers in 1815. Her contribution to the defeat of Napoleon included subsidies to her continental allies, Nelson's victories over the French fleet and the Duke of Wellington's successful land campaigns, culminating in the battle of Waterloo. For the next half-century Britain continued to play a prominent role in international affairs, participating in diplomatic conferences through which the powers tried to resolve major problems by negotiation rather than war.

   A major influence on British foreign policy was suspicion of Russia's designs on Constantinople, the capital of the Ottoman Empire, which was regarded as the 'key to India'. This was partly because of its proximity to the overland trade routes to the east and partly because it was feared that if Russia occupied Constantinople, she would be able to dominate the Near East. British ministers therefore supported the declining Ottoman Empire as a buffer against Russian expansion in the Near East. The Crimean War of 1854–56 was fought mainly to check Russian influence over Turkey. But Britain was disillusioned by the discrepancy between the heavy sacrifices made and the meagre results of the war, and turned against active involvement in European conflicts. This mood, combined with suspicion of Napoleon III's motives, largely explains why Britain was mainly a passive spectator of Bismarck's three wars in the 1860s, even though they profoundly affected the balance of power in Europe.

The recovery of world trade in the 1850s also tended to divert British attention away from Europe towards more distant parts of the world. As the 'first industrial nation', Britain enjoyed many advantages over her continental rivals for several decades, enabling her to expand her trade worldwide.

Between 1870 and 1914, Britain became the greatest imperial power in the world. With colonial possessions scattered across the globe, hers was 'the empire on which the sun never set'. During these same years, Britain lost her pre-eminence as a manufacturing nation, being overtaken by the USA and Germany. But Britain's reliance on imported food and raw materials, and the need for markets for her manufactured goods, meant that the nation's lifeblood was dependent on the uninterrupted flow of seaborne trade.

* Britain therefore needed to 'rule the waves'. To ensure that the sea lanes remained open to merchant shipping, Britain had to maintain her naval supremacy. The acquisition of coaling stations and naval bases was a necessary aspect of commercial and imperial expansion. Fears that Britain's navy was not adequate for the country's needs led to the Naval Defence Act of 1889, which established the principle of the 'Two Power Standard'. This meant that the Royal Navy was to be as large as the combined fleets of the next two naval powers.

The army played a much less conspicuous role in sustaining Britain's position as a great power. As the only European power that did not introduce conscription after 1871, Britain lacked the mass army of her continental rivals. Furthermore, much of the British army was either deployed in the defence of India or was scattered throughout the rest of the empire. Although the reputation of the British army suffered from the disastrous experience of the Boer War of 1899–1902, her military forces had performed well in colonial campaigns until then.

Britain had a well-established parliamentary system of government, which was democratised by stages in the nineteenth century. The monarch reigned but did not rule – a very different situation from that of imperial Germany. The aristocracy still played a very prominent part in politics and public service, as well as participating in the world of business, but they shared power and influence with the prosperous middle class. This was a much more open and meritocratic society than Germany's. Serious social problems existed in late nineteenth century Britain and labour unrest became intense at times, but the British political system seemed much better adapted to containing these stresses than its German counterpart. One important difference between the two systems was the simple fact that in Britain, the government of the day had to command a majority in parliament (especially in the House of Commons) to continue in office. Governments therefore took careful note of the views of MPs as well as of the press and the public. MPs tended to be particularly critical of government expenditure (since they and their constituents were taxpayers) which led to attempts to acquire empire 'on the cheap'.

   * British foreign policy naturally reflected, in part, her interests as a commercial and imperial nation. Immense importance was attached to safeguarding the route to India so that Suez and the Cape were regarded as areas of strategic concern. The defence of India itself, threatened by Russia's expansion into Central Asia, was also a major anxiety. Since the navy was incapable of sailing up the Khyber Pass, the riposte to a Russian threat to India was to consider sending a fleet into the Black Sea, to threaten Russia's vulnerable southern coastline.

   Traditionally, Britain also had been concerned to prevent any one power from dominating the European continent, as shown in the era of Napoleon, but from the mid-1860s to about 1900, the balance of power in Europe was not an important influence on British policy. This was the period of so-called 'Splendid Isolation' when British ministers were glad to be free of 'entangling alliances'. Nevertheless, Britain continued to be involved in European affairs, especially those relating to the Ottoman Empire and the Straits – the strategic waterway linking the Mediterranean and the Black Sea. By the turn of the century, however, many British statesmen were becoming convinced that Britain's resources were overstretched and that she needed allies if she were to maintain her role as a world power.

5 Austria-Hungary

From 1815 to 1848, the Austrian Chancellor, Metternich, exercised great influence in Europe, working closely with Russia and Prussia in an informal conservative alliance opposed to revolutionary movements. In 1854, however, Austria gave diplomatic support to Britain and France in the 'Crimean Coalition' against Russia, a sign that Austria was becoming more concerned about the fate of the Ottoman Empire and the Balkans. This trend was accelerated by her territorial losses in north Italy and exclusion from influence in Germany, resulting from her defeat in the 'war of liberation' of 1859 and the Austro-

Prussian war of 1866. In 1867, a new constitution was issued, granting a form of self-government to Hungary.

By 1871, Austria-Hungary was almost an anachronism, a multinational state in an age of growing nationalism, while her status as a great power had been weakened in the course of the unification of Italy and Germany. After 1871, her decline relative to other great powers continued. The economic progress she made was dwarfed by that of other countries, while political problems hampered her development as a modern efficient state. As a result of such weaknesses, she lacked the military power to play a fully independent role in international affairs.

* Austria-Hungary, sometimes called the 'Dual Monarchy', consisted of two separate states. The kingdom of Hungary (then more than twice its present size) had its own government and parliament at Budapest. The rest was 'Austria', consisting of the original Germanic heartland of the Habsburg dynasty and other lands acquired at various times populated by Czechs, Poles, Italians and others. These peoples has their parliament at Vienna, the old capital of the former Austrian Empire. A further complication was the curious system of 'Common Ministers' for the army, foreign policy and for deciding tariff policy. In addition, the consent of both prime ministers was necessary on major issues affecting Austria and Hungary. The Dual Monarchy was a ramshackle empire that was rather inadequately governed with a cumbersome bureaucracy.

The fundamental problem was that of cohesion. There were problems of co-ordinating the policies and resources of the two states as well as the major issue of how to bind the nationalities together. The scale of the problem can be seen from the fact that mobilisation posters had to be printed in 15 separate languages! The Emperor, Franz Joseph, was popular and well-intentioned, but conflicts between the nationalities were endless. Concessions to one group only provoked protests or riots by another, making parliamentary government impossible in Austria. In Hungary the dominant nation, the Magyars, ignored the claims of 'inferior' peoples, such as Slovaks, Croats and Serbs. The intermingling of peoples meant that the nationalities problem was virtually insoluble, but the policy of 'Magyarisation' in Hungary had great significance because it alienated the traditionally loyal Croats as well as the Serbs. The result was a Serbo-Croat alliance within Austria-Hungary that looked beyond the borders of the state to the independent kingdom of Serbia as a means of escape from Magyar oppression. The 'south Slav' problem, as it was called, threatened Austria-Hungary with disintegration.

* By 1871, she regarded the Balkans as a vital sphere of political influence and economic activity. This raised the problem of whether to oppose Russia or co-operate with her in Balkan issues. In 1871, Austrian hopes of an anti-Russian alliance with Germany conflicted

with Bismarck's desire for good relations with Russia. In order to check Russian influence, Austrian policy was directed towards creating client states in the Balkans and propping up the Ottoman Empire. Co-operation with Britain in the 'Eastern Question' was another option that served Austria-Hungary well for a time. The growth of nationalism in the Balkan states, particularly after 1900, raised serious problems for her. The most serious was Serbian hostility, backed by Russia.

6 Russia

Tsarist Russia was a powerful reactionary force in European affairs in the first half of the nineteenth century. She also enjoyed great prestige as a military power after Napoleon's disastrous Moscow campaign in 1812. The 'Holy Alliance' proposed by Alexander I in 1815 (in one of his brief flirtations with liberalism) soon came to be synonymous with repression and the defence of monarchical authority throughout Europe. After the upheavals of 1848, the Tsarist regime – the only sizeable continental state impervious to the revolutionary fever – seemed once again to overshadow Europe, resuming the role of arbiter in the affairs of Germany.

Russia's defeat in the Crimean War of 1854–56 was therefore a shattering blow to the prestige of Tsardom and a source of deep humiliation to Russia, which had important results in both domestic and foreign affairs. Within Russia, it inspired an attempt to modernise the local government, the army and educational system, as well as the abolition of serfdom in 1861. The effect on Russian foreign policy was equally dramatic. From being the defender of the status quo, Russia became a 'revisionist' power – facilitating political changes in Europe in the hope of opportunities to abrogate the deeply-resented Black Sea clauses of the 1856 Treaty. Austria's 'treachery' in siding with the western powers in 1854 was repaid by Russia's neutral stance when Napoleon III, and later Bismarck, declared war on the Austrian Empire in 1859 and 1866. Her opportunity to denounce the 1856 Treaty came during the Franco-Prussian war.

Russia was both a European and an Asiatic power. From the 1860s Russian rule was being extended over Central Asia to the Far East. This mainly affected her relations with Britain because of the threat to India and to Britain's commercial interests in China.

But Russia was a colossus with feet of clay, as her defeat by Japan in the war of 1904–5 demonstrated. Enormous in extent, with a population (in European Russia) in 1910 equal to that of Germany and Austria-Hungary combined, Russia was making great strides towards overcoming her backwardness compared with the other great powers. Rapid industrialisation in the 1890s, yielding the highest annual rate of increase in industrial production in the world (admittedly from a low base), produced an impressive expansion of heavy industry and of the railway network so that Russia was acquiring many of the trappings of a modern state. But a number of serious weaknesses prevented her from realising her full potential as a great power.

* Firstly, the Russian economy did not generate enough taxable wealth to meet the increasing needs of the state. Russian agriculture remained generally unproductive but grain from the richer regions had to be exported to pay for imported machinery for her industries. Industrialisation was also partly financed by massive foreign loans, but they increased the size of the state debt. If the peacetime army and navy was a heavy burden on the treasury, war itself was a luxury Russia could not afford. The war with Japan virtually bankrupted the state. Secondly, the persistence of widespread social and political discontent weakened the fabric of society and the state. Finally, one reason why such problems were not tackled more successfully was that the government was so incompetent. The Tsars clung to their autocratic powers, insisting on their divine mission, but they were quite incapable of ruling effectively. When a parliament, the *Duma*, was eventually permitted in 1905, it had little power to influence the government. On top of this, the Russian bureaucracy was notoriously corrupt and incompetent.

It is hardly surprising, therefore, that Russia was not the great military power that her size and resources suggested. Nor was it a coincidence that defeat was followed by revolution in 1905. The arbitrary nature of the Tsarist system of government also contributed directly to the unpredictability of Russian foreign policy, since the Tsar could be persuaded by individuals or groups to abandon the more cautious policies advocated by the foreign ministry.

* The formation of a united Germany in 1871, altering the political situation in Central Europe and creating a powerful neighbour on her western frontier, caused Russia considerable concern. In the Bismarck era (1871–90), Russia was content to work in association or alliance with Germany. The non-renewal of the alliance after Bismarck's fall led to an alliance with France, as a guarantee of security. This was not a very 'close' alliance, however, in that both sides had reservations about supporting the other on some issues and the Russians were tempted to renew their ties with Germany.

Russian policy towards the Ottoman Empire was a curious mixture of practical politics and romanticism. Control of the Straits, linking the Black Sea with the Mediterranean, would safeguard her economic and strategic interests. Unrestricted passage of merchant shipping through the Straits was vital to Russian trade, especially the export of grains from the Black Sea ports. The idea of recovering Constantinople from the Turks, on the other hand, was a dream that had excited the Russian imagination for over a century. However impracticable, the idea still influenced Russian policy at various times.

The official policy, pursued by the foreign ministry, was a cautious one, recognising that the 'Eastern Question' was a European question, a matter of concern to all the great powers. Russia would simply try to exploit favourable situations to secure advantages for herself or her protégés in the Balkans. Pan-Slavists, a motley collection of journalists, writers and generals, who believed Russia's 'destiny' lay in the Balkans, accepted no such restraints. They saw Russia's mission as the liberation of the Balkan Christians from Turkish oppression and the creation of independent Slav states under the protection of Mother Russia and the Orthodox Church.

A clash between Russia and Austria-Hungary over the Balkans was more or less inevitable, since Russian encouragement of Slav nationalism and her desire to weaken the Ottoman Empire spelt ruin for Austria-Hungary. Britain would also intervene if Russia was seen to have designs on the Straits or Constantinople. A new factor in the 1890s was the growth of German influence in Turkey as part of her economic penetration into the Near East. These conflicting ambitions could best be kept in check by the survival of the Ottoman Empire, 'the great shock-absorber of the European states system'.

7 The Ottoman Empire

The Ottoman Empire was a great military empire in decline – 'the sick man of Europe', in a well-worn phrase. Only partly European, it was a multi-national empire stretching from the borders of Austria-Hungary and Russia through the Balkans into Asia Minor, Persia and Arabia and through Egypt along the coast of north Africa. By 1870, the Sultan's authority in many parts of his empire was only nominal. Integration of Turks, Slavs and others in European Turkey had never been systematically attempted. The races and religions, Muslim and Christian, simply co-existed, usually in a state of mutual animosity, until grievances provoked uprisings. The revolts might be directed against Muslim landowners or against the Turkish authorities, and were sometimes accompanied by ferocious slaughter on both sides. This in turn usually resulted in some form of intervention by the European great powers.

Throughout the nineteenth century, the 'Eastern Question' – the problems arising from the expectation that, as a British minister expressed it in 1830, 'this clumsy fabric of barbarous power will speedily crumble into pieces from its own inherent causes of decay' – caused a series of crises in international affairs. The decline, or possible disintegration of the Ottoman Empire, carried with it the danger of conflict amongst the great powers. Crises occurred when

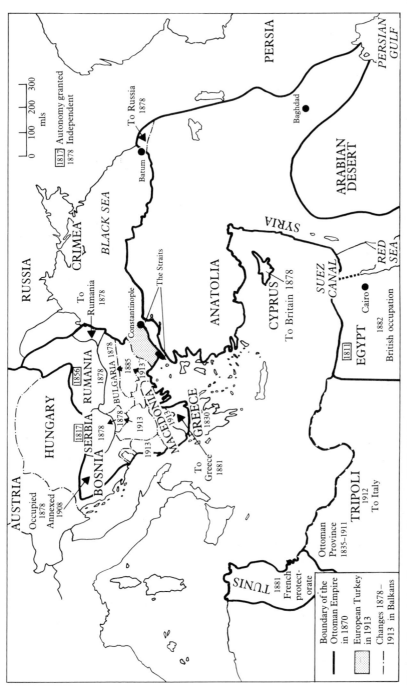

The decline of the Ottoman Empire, 1870–1913

either the interests or the particular areas of concern of one of the powers were infringed by someone else. This could be by one of the other powers or by one of their clients among the Balkan states, or by the Ottoman government itself.

★ There was no simple solution to the Eastern Question in the period 1871 to 1914. Partition of the Turkish empire would probably result in war because there was little hope of agreement on how to divide it amongst the powers. An alternative was to assist the Balkan states to obtain autonomy (self-government) or even complete independence from Turkey, as Greece, Serbia, Montenegro and Rumania had done earlier in the century. This solution was favoured by Russia, but opposed by Austria-Hungary. British governments also doubted the wisdom of weakening Turkey's ability to act as a barrier to Russian expansion into the Balkans or towards Constantinople and the Straits. The only other alternative was to 'prop-up' the Ottoman Empire in order to postpone its collapse, while putting pressure on the Turkish government to introduce reforms to improve the lot of its Christian subjects. This was the policy favoured by the majority of the powers, to which Russia reluctantly adhered at times. The attitudes of the powers, however, were liable to change according to the nature of the crisis. They were not always very consistent either – claiming to support the Ottoman Empire did not stop Britain or Austria-Hungary from acquiring Turkish territory!

In fact, Turkish sovereignty over European Turkey had been steadily eroded for over a century by the great powers, who claimed rights of protection over their co-religionists or special privileges for their resident nationals. Throughout the nineteenth century, the Turkish economy was subjected to increasing exploitation by European commercial groups, backed by their governments, who secured concessions for mining, manufacturing or transport facilities. Further-more, in 1881, a largely European debt administration was set up to supervise the Turkish finances, following a declaration of bankruptcy.

Widespread resentment amongst the Muslim population at this sort of European interference (which 'westernising' ministers had encouraged) led to a dramatic change in government. Abdul Hamid II re-established his authority as the Sultan (from 1876 to 1909) and re-asserted traditional Muslim values. But with a corrupt and ineffective system of government, the Empire could do little more than fight a rearguard action against both nationalist movements from within and European interference from without. Fear of dismemberment of the Empire was quite strong, for the actions of the great powers did not always match their professed policy of maintaining the integrity of the Ottoman Empire. Abdul Hamid's attempt to check the interference of the other great powers by encouraging German influence (for example, the Berlin-Baghdad railway) in the 1890s was only a partial success.

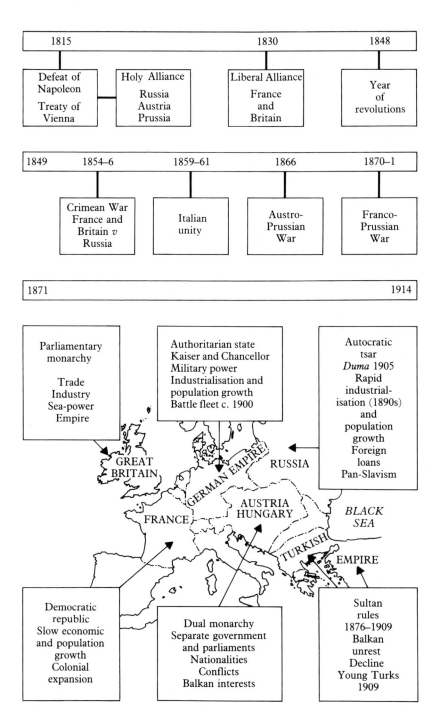

1815		1830	1848
Defeat of Napoleon Treaty of Vienna	Holy Alliance Russia Austria Prussia	Liberal Alliance France and Britain	Year of revolutions

1849	1854–6	1859–61	1866	1870–1
	Crimean War France and Britain *v* Russia	Italian unity	Austro-Prussian War	Franco-Prussian War

1871		1914

Parliamentary monarchy

Trade
Industry
Sea-power
Empire

Authoritarian state
Kaiser and Chancellor
Military power
Industrialisation and
population growth
Battle fleet c. 1900

Autocratic
tsar
Duma 1905
Rapid
industrial-
isation (1890s)
and
population
growth
Foreign
loans
Pan-Slavism

GREAT
BRITAIN

GERMAN EMPIRE

RUSSIA

FRANCE

AUSTRIA
HUNGARY

BLACK
SEA

TURKISH

EMPIRE

Democratic
republic
Slow economic
and population
growth
Colonial
expansion

Dual monarchy
Separate government
and parliaments
Nationalities
Conflicts
Balkan interests

Sultan
rules
1876–1909
Balkan
unrest
Decline
Young Turks
1909

Summary – Europe and the Great Powers

The 'Young Turk' revolution of 1909 was a desperate attempt to rejuvenate the Empire. By modernising the country and creating a more liberal form of government, modelled on European examples, the Young Turks hoped to persuade the great powers to desist from interference in Turkish affairs. Their claim to be regarded as 'the Japan of the Near East' (a successful modernising Asiatic state) fell on deaf ears. Only a few years after the Young Turks came to power, the Balkan states joined together and inflicted a crushing defeat on the Turkish army. By 1913, European Turkey had been reduced to a mere fraction of its size in 1870. Within a decade, the Ottoman Empire itself had ceased to exist.

Making notes on 'Europe and the Great Powers'

As you read this introductory chapter, you should be aware that sections 2 to 7, on the European powers and Turkey, serve a dual purpose. Firstly, they give a brief summary of developments from 1815 to 1870. Secondly, they present a more analytical treatment of aspects of the domestic situation (political and economic) which influenced the foreign policy of the powers in the period 1871 to 1914, some key points of which are referred to. Try to identify the strengths and weaknesses of each state and note any particular issues or regions which were of concern to them. Consider how far this chapter enables you to answer these questions: What grouping of the European states would produce a 'balance of power' in 1871? Would that grouping require some states to change their traditional alignments? In what ways did the 'balance of power' change between 1871 and 1914? Your notes could be quite brief, as essay questions are not normally asked on the subject matter of this chapter.

The following headings and sub-headings should provide a basic framework:
1.   The Franco-Prussian War
1.2. The European implications of it
2.   Germany
2.1. Bismarck's position 1871–90
2.2. German industrialisation
3.   France
3.1. Changes in French foreign policy, 1871–1914
4.   Great Britain
4.1. Importance of sea-power
4.2. Trade and strategy
5.   Austria-Hungary
5.1. Structure of the Dual Monarchy
5.2. Importance of the Balkans
6.   Russia

CHAPTER 2

Bismarck and Europe, 1871–90

1 1871–75

Germany's triumph over France in 1871, following her earlier victories over Denmark and Austria, made her the greatest military power on the continent. It also upset the existing balance of power in Europe. There was consequently considerable fear and suspicion that the new German Empire might continue to pursue an aggressive foreign policy. Bismarck, however, harboured no further expansionist designs. In his view, Germany was now a 'satiated' power. 'Any policy of German conquest', he dismissed as 'a piece of folly beyond all political reason'. Having achieved his major aim of creating a Prussian-dominated German state, his main objective was the security of the German Empire. The best guarantee of this was European peace.

   * The two obvious threats to Germany's desire for peace were a French war of revenge and an Austro-Russian conflict arising from the Balkans. France without allies did not pose a serious danger to Germany since Bismarck was confident that the German army could defeat her again, if necessary. But Germany's geo-political situation in Europe, sandwiched between France in the west and Russia in the east, made her peculiarly vulnerable to a war on two fronts. It was the possibility of a coalition including France that constituted the gravest menace to Germany's security. Another danger that Bismarck feared at times was a revival of the 'Crimean Coalition' of 1854 (Britain, France and Austria) which would leave Germany in an exposed position.

   Bismarck's solution to the two-fold problem was to try to isolate France and to reduce friction between Austria-Hungary and Russia over the Balkans, where their interests were often at variance. Until the Eastern Question reached an acute stage in 1877, however, Bismarck could adopt a 'low profile' approach to international problems. In 1878, however, circumstances forced him to accept that Berlin, the German capital, must become the pivot of European diplomacy. In practice, this meant that he would encourage the other great powers (France excepted) to feel dependent on Germany's goodwill and seek to neutralise their antagonisms by a 'balancing of discontents'. But, of course, Bismarck's objective was not to eliminate these antagonisms – that would have the undesirable effect of making them independent of Germany and even free to conspire against her. Bismarck's diplomacy was consequently something of a delicate balancing act, in which he sought to influence the relationships of the great powers towards Germany and towards each other.

   In 1871, Bismarck's immediate concern was to reassure the leaders of Europe that he was now genuinely a man of peace. Assurances to this effect, made through normal diplomatic channels, were reinforced by personal contacts between the German Kaiser, the Habsburg Emperor and the Tsar of Russia in the summer of 1871. The outcome of these monarchical gatherings was the Three Emperors' Agreement (*Dreikaiserbund*) of October 1873, initially an Austro-Russian treaty to which the Kaiser later gave his adherence. Although this Agreement was not of Bismarck's making, it suited his purposes well enough.

The content of the *Dreikaiserbund* of 1873 was somewhat vague. It expressed the desire of the three emperors to stand together in the interests of monarchical solidarity against the supposed threat from revolutionary socialism, following the Paris Commune of 1871. They also wished to reduce the risks of war arising from Austro-Russian differences over the Balkans. Hence the promise 'to consult together so that these divergences do not take precedence over considerations of a higher order' – that is, peace and stability.

In 1875, Bismarck's strategy of quietly allaying fears about Germany's dominant position in Europe was suddenly discarded in a crisis with France which he himself provoked. In April, the *Berlin Post* published an article (regarded as government-inspired) under the dramatic heading: 'Is War in Sight?' Contemporaries, as well as later historians were puzzled by this incident. It seemed that Bismarck was raising the spectre of war – but for no good reason and with no clear purpose. He may have been genuinely anxious at France's surprisingly rapid recovery from her defeat in 1871. The German General Staff was certainly concerned about the nature of the reorganisation of the French army. They misinterpreted it, believing the new system represented a big increase in the size of France's armed forces, and began to talk of the need for a preventive war.

Bismarck himself seems to have calculated that a diplomatic warning would be enough to discourage the French from further military expansion, but his methods were remarkably clumsy. The crisis backfired when France secured promises of support from Britain and Russia against German threats. The 'War in Sight' crisis demonstrates that Bismarck had been slow to adapt his diplomatic methods to suit Germany's dominant position in Europe which required her leaders to act with restraint.

2 The Near East Crisis, 1875–78

The Eastern Crisis began in 1875 with a rising against Turkish misgovernment in Bosnia and Herzegovina. The long-standing animosity of Christian peasants towards the oppressive rule of Muslim landowners was heightened by grievances over taxation and labour services. In 1876, the revolt spread to Bulgaria, then part of the Ottoman Empire, supported by the semi-independent states of Serbia and Montenegro.

The re-opening of the Eastern Question presented Bismarck with a major test of his statesmanship. Determined to avoid taking sides in disputes over the Balkans, he had somehow to convince both Vienna and St Petersburg of Germany's goodwill. If he failed, either Austria-Hungary or Russia might seek support from another power, Britain or France. There was no simple solution to the problem of conflicting Austro-Russian interests in the Balkans. From the Austrian point of view, the main danger lay in Russian encouragement of Slav nationalism. This was not only a threat to the integrity of the Ottoman Empire, in whose survival Austria-Hungary had a vested interest, but it also threatened the stability of the multi-national Habsburg Empire. In the case of Russia, the temptation to 'fish in trouble waters' in the hope of weakening Turkey was hard to resist. In addition, Russia, as the leader of the Orthodox Church, was under a moral obligation to aid the Christian Slavs if their Muslim Turkish rulers treated them too oppressively. Although Germany herself was not directly involved in Balkan disputes, she had good reason to be anxious at their effect on Austro-Russian relations.

Since Bismarck's 'solution' – partition of the Ottoman Empire – was unacceptable to the other powers, his options were limited. One of these was to seek British co-operation in dealing with the crisis. His dilemma in trying to reconcile Austro-Russian differences is well illustrated in this extract from a conversation between Bismarck and the British ambassador at Berlin (Lord Odo Russell) in January 1876, as reported to the foreign secretary (Lord Derby) in London.

1   Alone, without the support of England, he would not resist the annexing tendencies of Austria and Russia in Turkey because he did not think either of those Powers would be strengthened by such increase of territory, or the interests of Germany affected
5   by it. On this question he would, however, reserve his opinion until he knew that of HMG (Her Majesty's Government) and through HMG he also hoped to know what the French Government might be disposed to do. He would be glad to see France take again a lively interest in oriental matters which
10   might turn her attention from brooding over a war of revenge against Germany. He would also welcome the co-operation of Italy. If he could thus obtain for Germany the good will of England and her friends he could look to the future with greater confidence.
15   Germany could not well afford to let Austria and Russia become too intimate behind her back – nor could she let them quarrel with safety to herself. In the event of a quarrel between them, popular opinion and sympathy would probably side with Austria, which would make a rancorous and dangerous enemy
20   of Russia, who would then find a willing ally in France to injure Germany.

If on the other hand Germany took the part of Russia the
consequences might be fatal to the very existence of Austria,
who would go to pieces like a ship on a sandbank.

There remained neutrality – but neutrality would be impossible
25 for Germany if her allies quarrelled, and would involve a loss
of time Germany could not incur as matters stood.

All these considerations he wished to submit confidentially to
HMG and to solicit an exchange of views in return, in the hope
of being able to co-operate with England for the maintenance of
30 European peace. . .

Nothing came of this attempt to secure British co-operation, partly
because London waited in vain for specific proposals from Berlin.
Bismarck's continuing 'low profile' approach during the crisis worked
well enough until the end of 1877. Up to then his role was limited to
encouraging the Austrians and Russians to find an agreed solution to
the problem, while simultaneously pressing Britain to take the lead
in resisting Russia. In early 1878, however, the deepening crisis
obliged him to offer his services as 'honest broker' – a role he had
firmly rejected in 1876 for the reasons shown in this letter to state
secretary von Bülow:

1 The Three Emperors' Alliance has so far been a guarantee of
peace; if it is weakened and broken up because of the elective
affinities (mutual attraction) of Austria and England or Russia
and France, the incompatibility of Austro-Anglo-Russian interests
5 in the East will lead to war. Day after day Germany will be
called upon to be the arbitrator between the two hostile groups
of the Congress, the most thankless task that can fall to our lot;
and as we are not disposed firmly and from the outset to attach
ourselves to one of the two groups, the prospect is that our three
10 friends, Russia, Austria and England, will leave the Congress
with ill feeling towards us, because none of them has had the
support from us that he expected. A further danger to peace lies
in the direct contact into which Prince Gorchakov and Lord
Beaconsfield (Disraeli) would be put, two ministers of equally
15 dangerous vanity. . .

A novel feature of the Eastern Crisis of 1875–78 was the attempt
to turn localised discontents into a Slav crusade against the Turks,
itself a clear sign of the growth of nationalist feeling in the Balkans.
Also unusual was the sheer ferocity with which the two sides
slaughtered each other. The most notorious example was the 'Bulgarian
Atrocities' (1876) – the retaliatory massacre of allegedly over 10 000
Bulgarians by the Turks. These atrocities stirred public opinion in
both Britain and Russia, with important political effects. In Britain,
the Liberals' campaign against the 'Bulgarian Horrors' temporarily
prevented the Conservative government under Disraeli from pursuing

the traditional British policy of supporting Turkey against Russia. In Russia, the sufferings of the Balkan Christians enflamed Pan-Slavist sentiment to such an extent that the Tsarist government found itself under increasing pressure to intervene on the side of the Balkan rebels.

From 1875 to 1877 the great powers made a number of unsuccessful attempts to find a diplomatic solution to the Eastern Question. The most striking feature of this phase of the crisis was Austro-Russian co-operation, in keeping with the terms of the *Dreikaiserbund* of 1873. Although both states sought to extract some advantage for themselves from the situation, neither wanted to accelerate the collapse of the Ottoman Empire. Gorchakov, the ageing and conservative Russian foreign minister, recognised that Turkey's fate concerned all the great powers and favoured restraint. Andrassy, the Austro-Hungarian foreign minister, aware that German support was unlikely in the event of a clash with Russia, attempted to collaborate with the Russians.

Bismarck's main concern throughout the Eastern Crisis was to avoid an Austro-Russian confrontation in which Germany would have to take sides. The willingness of the foreign ministers of Austria-Hungary and Russia to co-operate in search of a solution was therefore a great relief to him. Even so, precautions were necessary in case of an Austro-Russian split, since at each new stage of the crisis the strains on the Austro-Russian accord increased. Bismarck's main strategem was to encourage Britain to play an active role in opposing Russia. 'England should entirely take the lead in the Eastern Question', Bismarck suggested, so as to reduce tension between his partners in the *Dreikaiserbund*. Britain was willing enough to fill this role because of her traditional suspicion of Russian designs on the Balkans and Constantinople, but was reluctant to oppose her single-handed.

* Despite Austro-Russian co-operation, the great powers failed to find a diplomatic solution to the crisis from 1875 to 1877. Although Austria-Hungary and Russia patched up a series of accords to cover the ever-changing situation in the Balkans, at least one of the other parties involved found reasons for rejecting every one of the proposed solutions. Thus the first proposal was rejected by the Balkan insurgents; a second was unacceptable to Britain; while yet another was rejected by the Turks. Proposals based on schemes to reform Turkish rule in the insurgent states were unacceptable to them if too limited in scope, but rejected by the Turks if more ambitious. Imposing a solution on Turkey, the only real way forward, was blocked by Britain's refusal to agree to coercion of the Sultan. This stemmed largely from the fear that weakening the Sultan's authority might lead to disintegration of the Ottoman Empire, from which Russia would gain the most. Given such restraints, there was not a lot of scope for finding a formula acceptable to all sides.

By the spring of 1877 Russia's patience was exhausted. Opinion in Russia had become increasingly restive as Serbs and Montenegrins faced defeat and Bulgars were subjected to ferocious reprisals by the Turks. At the news of the worsening plight of the Balkan Christians, 'Slavomania' spread throughout Russia. By 1877, several thousand Russian volunteers were fighting in Serbia, financed by a host of Slavic Committees. The Tsar's government was openly reproached by both the press and the clergy for failing in its 'holy duty' to aid the Christian Slavs.

Despite this pressure and the failure of the latest attempt at a diplomatic solution in January 1877, the Tsarist government still hesitated to declare war. With its finances in disorder after bad harvests and a severe depression, the government was reluctant to embark on a crusade from which Russia herself could expect little direct gain – in view of Austrian and British opposition to Russian expansion. In negotiations with Austria-Hungary in the spring of 1877, the Austrians had only agreed to remain neutral in a Russo-Turkish war if their Balkan interests were fully respected. Worse still, Britain made it plain that she would not tolerate sweeping Russian gains at Turkey's expense. Yet Turkish intransigence seemed to leave the Tsar's government little choice. As the war minister remarked: 'Russian honour forbids us to stand about any longer with lowered guns just for the sake of peace'.

When Serbia was defeated by the Turks, the Russians felt obliged to intervene. They declared war on Turkey in April 1877 but their progress was held up by the skilful Turkish defence of the fortress of Plevna. This had two significant consequences: firstly, it deprived the Russians of the chance of a quick victory; secondly, it caused British opinion to swing back in favour of the 'heroic little Turks'. Nevertheless, the Russians were able to resume their advance on Constantinople in January 1878. In the following month the Turks sued for peace and secured an armistice. Russia had undoubtedly won the war, but she proceeded to lose the peace. Intoxicated by success and Pan-Slavist enthusiasm, the Russian government extracted severe terms from Turkey in the Treaty of San Stephano in March 1878. European Turkey was to be reduced to small unconnected territories by the creation of a Greater Bulgaria, under Russian occupation for two years, while Russia herself made some useful territorial gains.

These terms confirmed Andrassy's worst fears that he had been duped. 'The Russians have played us false', he complained. The attitude of Germany and Britain was crucial in persuading the Russians to revise the peace treaty. Bismarck, however, had previously declared in December 1876 that German interests in the Balkans were not 'worth the healthy bones of a single Pomeranian musketeer' and in February 1878, he had offered his services as an 'honest broker', implying that he would not take sides in the dispute. The British attitude to the situation was much more positive. Troops were summoned from India and the fleet was despatched to Turkish waters,

The Balkans (1878–1881) and the Congress of Berlin

ready to sail into the Black Sea. Faced with Austro-British hostility and the threat of war, Russia agreed to a revision of the peace terms at an international conference to be held in Berlin in the summer of 1878.

3 The Congress of Berlin

Before the Congress met, much useful preparatory work had been done. The Russians agreed to the reduction of Greater Bulgaria in return for gains elsewhere. The Sultan promised to introduce reforms within the Ottoman Empire and to cede Cyprus to Britain, in exchange for a guarantee of his dominions in Turkey-in-Asia. Britain also agreed to back Austria-Hungary's claim to occupy Bosnia. Despite these preliminary accords, the Congress of the great powers which met in Berlin in June–July 1878 was not all plain sailing.

* The most contentious issue was the division of Greater Bulgaria. The Russian attempt to resist its partition (despite their earlier agreement) clashed with Britain's determination to limit the size of a Russian-dominated state. They only gave way when Disraeli resorted to the novel expedient of ordering his special train to be ready to leave Berlin at a few hours' notice. The Congress proceeded to divide Greater Bulgaria into three. The northern part, Bulgaria, was granted complete independence, under Russian supervision. To the south of Bulgaria, a province named Eastern Rumelia – to emphasise its separate existence – was to have a form of self-government under Turkish suzerainty. The third part, called Macedonia, was returned to Turkish rule (or misrule).

A number of other issues were decided in favour of the interests of the great powers. Russia recovered Bessarabia, which she had lost to Rumania in 1856 after the Crimean War. She also acquired Batum, a valuable port on the eastern edge of the Black Sea, from Turkey. The Turks objected strongly to the loss of Bosnia to the Austrians and were reluctant to cede Cyprus to Britain, but their protests were ignored. Russian objections were also ignored when Britain claimed the right (with the Sultan's assent) to send warships into the Black Sea whenever she judged it necessary. France, who had played a minor role during the crisis, made no territorial gains in 1878 but was encouraged to seek compensation in Tunisia – still under the nominal suzerainty of the Sultan of Turkey.

The Congress of Berlin reasserted the concept that the fate of Turkey was a matter of concern to all the great powers and could not be decided unilaterally, as Russia had attempted to do in the Treaty of San Stephano, described by one Russian diplomat as 'the greatest act of stupidity that we could have committed'.

* Most historians regard the Treaty of Berlin as only a temporary and limited solution of the Eastern Question. On the positive side, it can be said to have checked Russian domination of the Balkans, without a war amongst the great powers. The Sultan was also obliged to treat his Christian subjects more gently – for a time, at least. This apart, it is hard to see what the Congress 'settled'. The separation of Eastern Rumelia from Bulgaria was reversed within a decade, causing another crisis amongst the powers in 1885–88. Macedonia, restored to Turkish rule, became a source of constant unrest in later decades. Austrian rule in Bosnia had to be enforced by military action and was bitterly resented by both Turks and Serbs. The outright annexation of the province in 1908 also caused a major crisis. The Sultan evaded implementing serious reforms in Asia Minor which was the scene of new massacres in the 1890s. 'A rickety sort of Turkish rule', as Salisbury, the new British foreign secretary, called it, had been re-established in 1878 even though, as he admitted, 'it is a mere respite; there is no vitality left in them'. Nevertheless, the Ottoman Empire survived for another 40 years.

What were the alternatives? One was to allow Russia to dominate the Balkans. Another was to have put more faith in the ability of the Balkan peoples, especially the Bulgarians, to govern themselves. This was Salisbury's view when he subsequently remarked that 'we backed the wrong horse'. Some historians suggest that the great powers' neglect of the ambitions and claims of the smaller Balkan states was a fundamental defect of the Treaty of Berlin. Although Serbia, Rumania and Montenegro became fully independent states, their territorial gains were quite small. The great weakness of the Berlin settlement was that it postponed, rather than solved, most of the problems that it dealt with.

Bismarck was not to blame for this. In the course of the crisis he had advocated partition of the Ottoman Empire as the best solution. He favoured an east-west division of the Balkans between Russia and Austria-Hungary: Britain to take Egypt, while France should have Tunisia. When this failed, his main concern was to ensure that Britain, not Austria-Hungary, took the lead in opposing Russia. Although he performed well enough in his role of 'honest broker' at the Congress of Berlin, the Russians showed little gratitude for the support he gave to their interests.

The Congress of Berlin was certainly a sign of Germany's new power and influence in Europe. Bismarck's prestige as a statesman was also at its height, although the Congress cannot be seen as a great triumph for his policy. Germany had been reluctantly pushed into the limelight and was blamed by both sides for their disappointments, as these two comments by an Austrian delegate (Baron Schwegel) and a Russian diplomat (Shuvalov) suggest:

1 . . . Bismarck will certainly have declared to the Russians that he attaches greater importance to the gratification of our wishes than those of England – at the moment he is strikingly, even demonstrably, friendly with Andrassy; but I do not trust him
5 and I am convinced that basically he is only working for the Russians . . .

We discussed the enlargement of Montenegro and the Albanian question. Success was on our side, but the battle was fierce. England, France and Turkey sided with us, and Russia, Germany
10 and Italy were against, i.e. 4 against 3. German friendship seems at times very threadbare, and I see more and more clearly how honest are the western nations, the English and the French.

Shuvalov summed up his views as follows:

1 You may well ask why we have so far not obtained any better
results backed by the powerful goodwill of Bismarck. It is
because we have been confronted by systematic opposition
from England and Austria. Andrassy, very cordial, acting the
5 gentleman in his talks with me, becomes a different person when
in the presence of the English, and turns into a servile admirer
of every word that falls from the lips of Beaconsfield. The
consequence is that Bismarck, whose chief preoccupation is to
avoid clashes, and to bring the Congress to an end, finds himself
10 forced to tack between the three of them (including Gorchakov)
and does not always exert an energetic goodwill towards us . . .

The power most pleased with the Treaty of Berlin was undoubtedly
Britain. Important British interests in the Mediterranean, especially
her naval influence, had been safeguarded and she had acquired
Cyprus as a base to enable her to resist Russian expansion in Asia
Minor. She had even asserted a right to send warships into the Black
Sea whenever she judged it necessary. This virtual repudiation by
Britain of the 'Rule of the Straits' of 1841 caused the Russians great
alarm. Russian influence and her threat to Constantinople had been
checked. In addition, co-operation with Austria-Hungary had produced
useful results and the unity of the three eastern courts had been
broken. It was naturally this last point which caused Bismarck most
concern.

4 The Making of the Alliance System, 1879–84

* 1878 seems to mark a turning point in Bismarckian foreign policy.
Faced with Russia's hostility and fearing the creation of a coalition
against Germany, he changed his approach. From now on, he tended
to seize the initiative and attempt to influence events to ensure
Germany's security. This led to the creation of the 'Bismarckian
system' – 'an overall political situation in which all the powers except
France have need of us and are. . .kept from forming coalitions against
us by their relations with one another'.

Bismarck's anxieties for Germany's security were much increased
after the Congress of Berlin. The Tsar regarded the Congress as 'a
European coalition against Russia, under the leadership of prince
Bismarck'. Austria-Hungary was co-operating closely with Britain to
enforce the terms of the treaty on the Turks and the Russians. This
left Germany rather on her own and exposed to the full blast of
Russian hostility – spearheaded by the pro-French Pan-Slav faction
around the Tsar. His displeasure with Bismarck's attitude was made
abundantly clear to the Kaiser (whose sympathies were pro-Russian),
as this letter of August 1879 suggests:

" HUMPTY-DUMPTY " !

" HUMPTY-DUMPTY SAT ON A WALL ;
 HUMPTY-DUMPTY HAD A GREAT FALL:
 DIZZY, WITH CYPRUS, AND ALL THE QUEEN'S MEN,
 HOPES TO SET HUMPTY-DUMPTY UP AGAIN."

1 . . . The Turks, sustained by their friends the English and
Austrians, who in the meantime firmly hold two Turkish
provinces, invaded by them in times of peace . . . do not cease
to raise difficulties of detail which are of the greatest importance
5 as much for the Bulgars as for the brave Montenegrins. . . .
Decision rests with the majority of the European commissioners.
Those of France and Italy join ours on practically all questions,
while those of Germany appear to have received the word of
command to support the Austrian view which is systematically
10 hostile to us and is so in questions which in no way interest
Germany but are very important for us.
   Forgive, my dear Uncle, the frankness of my language based
on the facts, but I think it is my duty to call your attention to
the sad consequences which these may cause in our good
15 neighbourly relations by embittering our two nations against
each other, as the press of the two countries is already doing.

In 1878–79 it seemed to Bismarck that Germany was presented with
a stark choice between continuing Russian hostility or an alliance with
her. Despite the benefit to Germany's security that an alliance would
bring, Bismarck was unwilling to be dependent on Russia. The desire
for good relations with Russia, he insisted, 'could not extend so far
that German policy is permanently subordinated to Russian policy
and that we sacrifice our relationship with Austria for Russia's sake'.
His response to the pressure from Russia was to put out feelers for
an alliance with Austria-Hungary.

The actual proposal he put to Andrassy in 1879 was a curious one.
It envisaged a permanent relationship, creating a sort of 'Germanic
bloc' in Europe that covered threats from any quarter. As the junior
partner in the alliance, Austria-Hungary's Balkan ambitions would be
kept in check, while the exclusive tie with Germany would 'dig a
ditch' between the Austrians and the western powers. This type of
alliance would also complement Bismarck's plan for a Catholic-
Conservative majority in the *Reichstag*.

Andrassy flatly rejected these proposals. The idea of a 'Germanic
bloc' made no sense to the Hungarian-born foreign minister of a multi-
national state. What he wanted was a defensive pact directed solely
against Russia, which he achieved.

★ By the terms of the Dual Alliance of October 1879, the signatories
promised to give full support if either were attacked by Russia. If the
attack came from a power other than Russia, the ally was only required
to observe a benevolent neutrality. The anti-Russian direction of this
alliance is quite clear. The treaty was secret and to last initially for
five years, with provision for automatic renewal at 3 year intervals.
This treaty has been called a 'landmark' in European history by
Gordon Craig, on the grounds that:

1 While previous treaties had usually been concluded during or
   on the eve of wars, or for specific purposes and restricted
   duration, this peacetime engagement turned out to be a permanent
   one. . . It was, moreover, the first of the secret treaties, whose
5 contents were never fully known but always suspected, and
   which encouraged other powers to negotiate similar treaties in
   self-defence, until all Europe was divided into league and counter-
   league.

The terms of the Austro-German treaty were not ideal from
Bismarck's point of view, but it served his purpose well enough. The
Russians, getting wind of the negotiations, made known their desire
for a *rapprochement* with Germany even before the treaty was signed.
Bismarck seized upon this to create a new tripartite alliance, embracing
both Russia and Austria-Hungary. More than 18 months elapsed,
however, before the new *Dreikaiserbund* was signed in June 1881,
indicating that securing agreement to its terms taxed Bismarck's skills
to the utmost. The major problem, apart from delays caused by the
accession of a new Tsar, was Austria-Hungary's determined opposition
to the whole project. The foreign minister, Andrassy, alleged that
'Russia was full of perfidy'. In his view, the whole point of the Austro-
German alliance was that it was meant to be the 'tombstone' of the
old *Dreikaiserbund*, not a 'stepping stone' towards a new one. He
envisaged the alliance with Germany as the first step towards the
creation of a powerful anti-Russian bloc, embracing Britain and
possibly France. Austrian resistance persisted throughout 1880, until
a change in British policy towards Turkey made them despair of
continuing co-operation with her. They therefore yielded to Bismarck's
pressure to seek an understanding with Russia over the Balkans.

   * By the terms of the *Dreikaiserbund* of 1881, each member of the
alliance could count on the neutrality of their partners if it was at war
with another power. Germany was thus liberated from the danger of
a Franco-Russian combination directed against her. It was also agreed
that the allies would not allow territorial changes in European Turkey
without their mutual agreement. They would also 'take account of
their respective interests in the Balkans'. Thus Russia's insistence on
the closure of the Straits to warships (especially British) was asserted
and the eventual reunion of Bulgaria and Eastern Rumelia was
accepted. In return, Russia recognised Austria-Hungary's right to
annex Bosnia. The alliance was secret and was to last for three years.

Germany's security was greatly enhanced by this treaty which
liberated her from the danger of a Franco-Russian combination.
Occupying a pivotal role in the alliance, she could expect that both
her allies would become dependent on her. It also assured her of the
goodwill of the new Tsar, Alexander III, and thereby lessened the
danger to her of the Pan-Slav faction.

* The menace seemed quite real when a leading Pan-Slav general visited Paris in early 1882, campaigning for a Franco-Russian alliance. This incident made Bismarck feel uncertain about Russia's reliability. Accordingly, the Dual Alliance partners responded more favourably in 1882 to Italian approaches for an alliance, which they had previously rejected. Bismarck's encouragement of French ambitions in Tunisia had been based partly on the calculation that it would drive a wedge between France and Italy, who had designs herself on the same territory. His object, though, had been to increase France's isolation, not to draw Italy closer to Germany, for the simple reason that Italian ambitions (which were directed towards areas of no interest to Germany) were regarded as a liability. But in early 1882, the spectre of a Franco-Russian alliance made Italy seem a useful ally against France. Even so, the commitments undertaken were quite closely limited.

By the terms of the Triple Alliance of May, 1882, both Germany and Italy were entitled to support from each other against an unprovoked attack by France. In the event of an attack by two powers, all the partners would render mutual assistance. If Austria-Hungary were at war with Russia, Italy would be neutral – thus giving the Austrians security on their southern frontier. In this respect the Triple Alliance served as a useful adjunct to the Dual Alliance of 1879 with its anti-Russian emphasis but it did not, as is often said, convert the Dual Alliance of 1879 into the Triple Alliance. The network of alliances was further extended by treaties between Austria-Hungary and Serbia in 1881, and with Rumania in 1883. The following year, the *Dreikaiserbund* was renewed without difficulty for a further three years.

The years 1882 to 1887 marked the zenith of the Bismarckian system, when Bismarck could feel confident that Germany's position in Europe was quite secure. This enabled him to indulge in the luxury of colonial ventures in which he could even seek French co-operation against Britain in Africa.

5 Bismarck and Colonies, 1884–90

In 1884–85 the absence of serious difficulties with either Russia or France enabled Bismarck to embark on an energetic colonial policy. As a consequence, Germany acquired an overseas empire in various parts of Africa and consolidated her claims to a number of islands in the Pacific. Bismarck's interest in colonies, however, was fairly short-lived. In terms of size, her empire was quite modest by 1890, as well as being economically insignificant.

In the early 1880s, Bismarck had expressed opposition to acquiring colonies but by 1884 he decided that, after all, they might serve a useful political purpose as well as being of some benefit to the German economy. Industrialists were anxious for new markets for manufactured goods: trading companies were complaining of being squeezed out of parts of Africa by foreign rivals. In addition, well-established trading companies in Hamburg and Bremen were pressing for more active government support for their overseas activities.

When Bismarck decided to satisfy these demands for colonies, he assumed that they would be largely self-supporting financially. The government's responsibilities would therefore be limited to granting 'Reich Protection' to trading companies, such as the German East Africa Company. Banks and investors would provide the necessary funds to make the colonies economically viable. In this, he was to be disappointed. Most of Germany's colonies in Africa became a financial burden, partly because the leading banks saw them as a far from promising investment. Within a few years Bismarck was complaining that 'if commerce has no interest in keeping the colonies then neither have I'. Furthermore, native risings, provoked by insensitive colonial officials and grasping commercial interests, necessitated action by the German government. It is not surprising, therefore, that by 1889 Bismarck was complaining of being 'sick and tired of colonies'.

In addition, by this time colonial ventures had ceased to offer any more short-term political advantages and they had also become a liability in diplomatic affairs. In 1884–85 the situation had been quite different. Colonies had seemed a good issue to raise in the 1884 elections when colonialism caught the public mood. Colonial Societies were being founded and academics and journalists were campaigning for a German overseas empire as an expression of German power and prestige in the world. As well as cashing in on this public mood for the sake of popularity in general, Bismarck had a more specific objective. He needed an issue that would weaken the liberal parties in Germany who had gained strength in the 1881 elections. To bolster his own position as a conservative Chancellor, he also wanted to discredit the groups associated with the Crown Prince who personified the values of English-style liberalism – detested by Bismarck. For such a purpose, a colonial conflict with Britain was ideal – 'a stunt got up for the 1884 elections', as one of Bismarck's advisers later asserted. As such, it served its purpose very well. A colonial conflict with Britain offered another short-term advantage in diplomatic affairs – improving Franco-German relations by enlisting French support against Britain. There was also the possibility of a further benefit to be gained by putting pressure on Britain in the colonial field, since it might force her into adopting a more pro-German policy in European affairs.

Bismarck's colonial policy in 1884–85 was therefore deliberately anti-British. He asserted claims to territories in Africa, such as Togo, the Cameroons and South West Africa, that challenged existing British commercial or imperial interests. In East Africa he encouraged German traders to establish claims against their British rivals. In collaboration with France, he not only wrecked a conference on Egypt's financial problems but also challenged a rather dubious British manoeuvre to protect her interests in the Congo, insisting that rival claims in the region be submitted to an international conference (see p. 58). Bismarck achieved his objectives without difficulty because the British government was bewildered by Germany's unexpected change of front over colonies and also faced a sudden crisis in 1885 when Russia threatened Afghanistan. Hence, while her diplomatic position was so weak, she could not afford to antagonise Germany in colonial matters. In 1886 this worked to Germany's advantage when the two powers were defining the British and German spheres in East Africa.

Only a year later, however, the diplomatic tide had turned in Britain's favour. The Franco-German colonial entente had been replaced by a renewal of tension. More serious still, Russo-German relations were badly strained after a new crisis in the Balkans. By 1890, when a second partition agreement was being negotiated over East Africa, the roles were reversed compared with 1886. An official observed that 'a good understanding with England means much more to Bismarck than the whole of East Africa'. As a result, Germany made substantial concessions to Britain in this area.

Most historians agree that Bismarck's interest in colonial matters was short-lived and that his policy was subordinate to his assessment of the international situation. The main exception to this is Wehler, who argues that Bismarck used imperialism as a way of distracting attention from social problems in Germany – hence the phrase 'social imperialism'. The traditional view seems sounder. Thus, in 1884–85, when European affairs were favourable to Germany, he played the colonial game with great vigour. He seems to have become disillusioned with it remarkably quickly, however, and by 1888 he was resisting demands for further colonial expansion on the grounds of Germany's continental security. In a classic phrase he asserted: 'My map of Africa lies in Europe. Here is Russia and here is France, and we are in the middle'.

6 The Bismarckian System under Pressure, 1885–90

In 1885 a revolt broke out in Eastern Rumelia, in favour of union with Bulgaria. This demand contravened the Treaty of Berlin which, at Britain's insistence, had deliberately divided the two provinces on the assumption that Russia would dominate Bulgaria and thereby increase her influence in the eastern Balkans. The Russians, however, had created widespread resentment in Bulgaria in the early 1880s by treating it as a Russian satellite. As a result, the Bulgarians expelled all Russian officials. When, on top of this insult, the Prince of Bulgaria accepted the demands of the Rumelian movement for unity, the Tsar's indignation knew no bounds.

★ At a meeting of the representatives of the great powers, the Russians naturally condemned the revolt as a violation of the Berlin Treaty. Germany and Austria-Hungary supported her in accordance with their treaty obligations. Britain took a different line, suggesting that the two provinces be linked by a 'Personal Union' under the Prince of Bulgaria, a device by which Rumania had become united in the 1860s. Britain's *volte face* towards the issue of Bulgarian unity was obviously due to the fact that the Bulgars had thrown off Russian tutelage. An enlarged independent Bulgaria was expected to be better able to check Russian influence in the Balkans. The British proposal was eventually adopted when France and Italy decided to back it. The rule of the Bulgarian Prince, however, was short-lived when the Tsar got his revenge by forcing him to abdicate. But Bulgarian resistance to Russian pressure persisted, raising the threat of a Russian invasion to restore their influence. This was too much for Austria-Hungary. In November 1886, she warned the Russians against further interference in Bulgaria even though Germany would not support her.

Bismarck made clear his refusal to take sides in this dispute in a statement to the *Reichstag* in early 1887 saying, 'It is a matter of complete indifference to Germany who rules in Bulgaria and what becomes of her'. This statement of Germany's neutrality in the dispute was not enough to satisfy the Tsar, who made plain his refusal to renew the *Dreikaiserbund* which was due to expire in June. Bismarck feared that unless he made a positive gesture towards Russia, the Tsar might yield to Pan-Slavist pressure for an alliance with France. He therefore decided on a bold step – proposing a secret Russo-German alliance.

★ By the terms of this alliance, the Reinsurance Treaty of 1887, Germany recognised Russia's right to a preponderant influence in Bulgaria. She also agreed to Russian control of the Straits if her security required it. If either power was at war, the other would remain neutral – unless France or Austria-Hungary were the object of attack. This proviso was highly significant. The Russians had demanded a free hand to attack Austria-Hungary, which Bismarck naturally refused. In return, Germany forfeited the free hand to attack France which she had enjoyed under the 1881 alliance. Bismarck seemingly put such a high premium on Russia's friendship in 1887 that he was prepared to contravene the spirit, if not the letter, of the Austro-German alliance of 1879. That alliance, after all, had been directed specifically against Russia.

Bismarck's fears for Germany's security had grown considerably in late 1886 and early 1887. Russia and Austria-Hungary appeared to be on the brink of war over the Balkans. In addition, a spirit of *revanchism*

re-emerged in France, associated with the popular and politically
ambitious figure of General Boulanger. He seemed all too willing to
escalate a minor dispute with Germany into a major crisis. This led
to renewed speculation about a Franco-Russian alliance.

To add to Bismarck's difficulties, the Italians were demanding
greater recognition for their interests in the Mediterranean as the price
of renewing the Triple Alliance, due to expire in May 1887. This
problem was settled relatively easily. Both Germany and Austria-
Hungary made concessions, promising support for Italian interests in
North Africa and the Balkans. When the British government, in
response to Italian requests for reassurance against a French attack,
made a loose agreement with Italy and Austria-Hungary to defend the
status quo in the Mediterranean, a solution to the main problem facing
Bismarck began to emerge.

If Britain could be persuaded to play a more positive role in resisting
Russia in the Near East, Germany's predicament would be considerably
eased. One advantage could be that Russia might be restrained from
adopting too aggressive a stance over Bulgaria. Another was that
Austria-Hungary might find in London the sympathetic response to
her desire for support that she could not get from Berlin. Austrian
discontent with Germany's policy was expressed by her foreign minister
(Kalnoky) in August 1887, in the following terms:

1   What does us most harm at the moment in the east is the attitude
    of Germany in the Bulgarian question. It is quite true . . . that
    Prince Bismarck, faithful to his earlier attitude, supports the
    Russian plans concerning Bulgaria at Constantinople and has
5   advised the Sultan to come to an understanding with Russia,
    that is, to lead the Russians back to Bulgaria. This does not
    surprise me, and I was convinced that Bismarck will not change
    his russophile attitude as far as Bulgaria is concerned. On the
    other hand I doubt whether he will do more than remain
10 consistent in theory, but this is more than enough to jeopardise
    the influence of our group (the allies of the Mediterranean
    Agreement). It is not to be wondered at if this peculiar attitude
    of Germany vis-a-vis the Sultan is misunderstood and causes
    confusion and distrust. Only a short while ago Germany sided
15 with us, Italy and England against the action of France and
    Russia in the Egyptian question. A few weeks later Germany,
    together with France, supports the Russians in a course of action
    which is blatantly hostile to us . . . And yet it would not be
    true to believe that our alliance with Germany has been in any
20 way undermined – on the contrary, on the German side there
    is an even greater effort to foster and cherish this alliance as the
    only reliable prop and bastion against war and its advocates . . .
    It must be because of the very vulnerable position of Germany

between France and Russia that Bismarck keeps trying to
25 separate Russia from France by showing favour to the Emperor
Alexander in the Bulgarian question, in which he has such a
personal interest . . .

Bismarck revealed his views on the role he thought Britain should
play in this report of his conversation with the British ambassador in
Berlin in February 1887:

1 I made it clear to the English ambassador that in the present
situation we could do little more than hold France in check. But
if this is done, in the full sense of the word, it will allow England
as well as Italy greater freedom of movement, and if these two
5 powers in combination with Austria are seemingly strong enough
to prevent Russia from disturbing the peace, and if on the other
hand Germany and France so counterbalance each other that
one sword keeps the other in its scabbard, then equilibrium and
peace in Europe would be assured. Both depend solely on
10 England; but if England withdraws from that combination, then
we should be forced to seek other expedients already mentioned,
in order to do what we can on our side for the maintenance of
peace.
I repeatedly assured the English ambassador that we should
15 not attack France in spite of all Boulangist provocation . . . But
if England thinks she can sit back and leave us to settle alone
all questions on the continent, then there is always the danger
that one day . . . she may find herself having to face one of the
continental powers in isolation, simply because of her refusal to
20 take part in European politics. In the interest of Germany's
safety I consider it expedient to seek a *rapprochement* either with
England or Russia, if peace and equilibrium cannot be assured
by the constellation I have sketched above.

* The conclusion of the secret Reinsurance Treaty in June 1887
removed Bismarck's fears of a Franco-Russian alliance. It did not
necessarily reduce the danger of a clash over the Balkans, where the
Bulgarian situation continued to cause tension through the summer
and autumn of 1887. Having conceded Russia's ambitions there,
Bismarck cast around for a means of discouraging her from precipitating
a crisis. The fact that Britain and Italy proved to be staunch allies of
the Austrians, allowing Germany to remain in the background,
suggested a way out of the dilemma. Bismarck decided to capitalise
on this by exerting all his influence to encourage Britain to conclude
a formal agreement with Italy and Austria-Hungary to defend the
status quo in both the Mediterranean and the Near East. He expressed
Germany's interest in Britain's support for his allies in a letter to the
British foreign minister (Lord Salisbury) in November 1887:

1 Austria and England have loyally accepted the status quo of the
German Empire . . . France and Russia on the other hand seem
to be threatening us. . .
    Given this state of affairs we must regard as permanent the
5 danger that our peace will be disturbed by France and Russia.
Our policy therefore will necessarily tend to secure what alliances
we can in view of the possibility of having to fight our two
powerful neighbours simultaneously. . . .But war against France
and Russia allied, . . . would always be a sufficiently great
10 calamity for our country for us to try and avoid it by an amicable
arrangement with Russia, if we had to do it without an ally . . .
We shall avoid a Russian war as long as this is compatible with
our honour and security, and as long as the independence of
Austria-Hungary, whose existence as a great power is of
15 paramount importance for us, is not called into question. We
hope that the friendly powers who have interests to safeguard
in the east which we do not share will, both by alliance and
military force, become strong enough to keep Russia's sword in
its scabbard, or to resist, if circumstances lead to a rupture. As
20 long as German interests are not involved, we shall remain
neutral. . .
    (but) Germany would always be obliged to enter the fighting
line if the independence of Austria-Hungary were threatened by
Russian aggression, or if England or Italy ran the risk of being
25 invaded by the French. German policy will therefore follow a
course forcibly prescribed by the political situation in Europe.

This Second Mediterranean Agreement of December 1887 aimed
to check Russia in Bulgaria and at the Straits by the deployment of
Austrian troops and British warships, with Italian backing. This
combination deterred the Russians from resorting to force. A few
months later, they assured the Austrians of their peaceful intentions,
despite their setbacks in Bulgaria. Bismarck's worst fears of an Austro-
Russian clash had not been realised.

   * Despite the Reinsurance Treaty, Russo-German relations never
regained their former cordiality. Bismarck was partly to blame for
this. At the end of 1887, Russia was denied access to the Berlin money
market for loans to finance her industrialisation. This was a politically
movitated decision 'to bludgeon the Tsar into seeing where his interest
lies'. It misfired when Russia turned to Paris for loans, creating an
important link that developed a political dimension a few years later.

    The years 1888 to 1890, when Bismarck fell from office, saw some
questioning of the basic assumptions on which Bismarck's diplomacy
had been based, especially the importance of 'keeping open the wire
to St Petersburg'. The anti-Russian sentiments of the new Kaiser,
Wilhelm II, who acceded in 1888, were shared by many influential

people in Germany. Both industrial and agrarian groups regarded Russia's economic modernisation as a threat to their interests. In military circles there was serious talk of the need for a preventive war against Russia before she became too powerful.

   * Bismarck himself seems to have had doubts about the feasibility of a closer relationship with Russia as the answer to the problem of Germany's security. These doubts lay behind his proposal for an alliance with Britain, which he made in early 1889. Receiving a rather non-committal response, Bismarck allowed the proposal to lapse assuming that, for the time being, German diplomacy would operate on the basis of the existing alignments. The Kaiser, however, accepted the case made by his advisers against the renewal of the Reinsurance Treaty. Disagreement between him and Bismarck over the Russian alliance was one of the issues which led to Bismarck's resignation in 1890.

7 Bismarck's Foreign Policy, 1871–90: Success or Failure?

A statesman's success or failure is not something that can usually be measured with great precision, but historians have devised a number of yardsticks that can be helpful. The most obvious of these is how far a statesman achieved his aims. The complexities of the problems facing a leader are also relevant to an assessment of his achievements. In particular, the amount of choice, the options open to a statesman, should be taken into account. Another consideration is whether the policies pursued produced solutions that were lasting or only brought short term advantages.

   In the case of Bismarck's foreign policy, the aims are quite clear, as are the problems Germany faced. He made decisions from a limited number of options available to him. In the short term, his success was very great. Germany enjoyed security and Europe was blessed with peace for 20 years. By 1890, however, the 'Bismarckian system', based on an elaborate structure of alliances, appeared to be played out. This may indicate that Bismarck chose the wrong option in 1881 and that a better course could have been to reinforce the Austro-German alliance by seeking British support against Russia. Another weakness of Bismarckian diplomacy is that his frequent use of bluster and blackmail were self-defeating, creating a legacy of distrust. For example, P M Kennedy suggests that British ministers pursued a pro-German policy despite Bismarck, rather than because of him. This is hardly a resounding accolade for Germany's greatest statesman. Thirdly, historians have frequently questioned whether some of Bismarck's fears were not more imaginary than real. The best example of this is the way he over-reacted to talk of a Franco-Russian alliance, that 'nightmare of coalitions' as he called it. He seems to have exaggerated the actual force of *revanchism* in France and of Pan-Slavism in Russia, while failing to take account of Alexander III's aversion to the republican regime in France. Bismarck's reply to such comments made by a contemporary was fair enough: 'When one is answerable for the fate of a great empire, one must watch carefully for symptoms which hint at threats to it, and take counter action in good time'.

Although Bismarck succeeded in one of his basic aims – keeping France 'in quarantine' for twenty years – the French problem remained nonetheless insoluble. Bismarck's diagnosis of the situation made in 1872 was fundamentally sound: 'Our chief danger for the future', he said, 'will be the moment France is once again regarded by the royal courts of Europe as a potential ally'. The recovery of France from her defeat inevitably carried with it the threat of a war of revenge. This threat, however, was latent rather than active for most of the period 1871–90. Most Republican leaders were realistic enough to appreciate that France could not hope to reverse the verdict of 1871 single-handed.

Except for the War Scare of 1875, which Bismarck himself provoked, the only crisis in Franco-German relations was the Boulangist episode in 1887–89. When General Boulanger courted popularity by enflaming nationalist sentiment in France, Bismarck retaliated with bellicose speeches to warn the French government that its Minister of War was a dangerous liability. Boulanger's dismissal ended the tension. What seriously worried Bismarck in 1887 was not a handsome, but politically inept, French general playing to the crowd, but a flamboyant Pan-Slavist Russian general campaigning in Paris for a Franco-Russian alliance.

Bismarck believed that the answer to the French danger lay in St Petersburg and, to a lesser extent, in Vienna, rather than in London. If Russia and Austria-Hungary were drawn into Germany's orbit, the threat from France would be neutralised. This was achieved by means of the *Dreikaiserbund* of 1873 and 1881, the Austro-German Alliance of 1879 and the Reinsurance Treaty of 1887. France's isolation was completed by Italy's attachment to the German powers in the Triple Alliance of 1882 and the Anglo-French estrangement over Egypt (see p. 56).

* In one sense, therefore, Bismarck achieved complete success in his aim of separating France from the other powers. However, the price of keeping Russia and France apart rose between 1881 and 1887, as is shown by the favourable terms obtained by the Russians in the Reinsurance Treaty. The fact remains that despite this success, Bismarck could not effect a reconciliation with France. Alsace-Lorraine was a permanent, if latent, factor in Franco-German relations.

Bismarckian diplomacy was therefore conditioned from the outset by the fact that one of the five great powers could never become an ally of Germany and had to be regarded as a potential enemy. By 1886, Holstein, one of Bismarck's advisers, was complaining: 'We are literally immobilised by France'. Short of returning the 'lost provinces' to France, which was unthinkable, or a preventive war, which would not be tolerated by other powers, the problem was insoluble. When Russo-German relations were strained, Bismarck's room for manoeuvre was very limited. It seems legitimate, therefore, to suggest that an alternative strategy – an alliance with Britain – might have been a better policy for dealing with the problem of France, as well as that of Austro-Russian relations.

The success of Bismarck's strategy for isolating France, as well as his hopes of reducing Austro-Russian tension in the Balkans, depended on maintaining Russian goodwill. The difficulties he encountered over this are shown by his attempt to play the role of 'honest broker' at the Congress of Berlin, which earned him the ingratitude of both the Austrians and the Russians who were dissatisfied with the final settlement. The persistence of Russian hostility in 1878–79 led him to seek an alliance with Austria-Hungary.

There is some uncertainty amongst historians, however, about Bismarck's motives in seeking this alliance. He may have intended the alliance with Austria-Hungary in 1879 to be merely the first stage towards the formation of the alliance of 1881 which included Russia. The Three Emperors' Agreement of 1881 satisfied Bismarck's formula of being 'one of three in an unstable equilibrium of five powers'. This tripartite alliance could be seen, therefore, as Bismarck's real objective from 1878 onwards because it neutralised two anti-German forces, French *revanchism* and Russian Pan-Slavism.

The main flaw in this interpretation is that it fails to take account of the actual nature of the alliance that Bismarck initially made with the Austrians. It was to be based on the 'Germanic ties' linking the two states, a concept that could hardly be expanded to include a non-German state such as Russia. But when the Austrians rejected this idea, insisting on a more conventional treaty, it is understandable that Bismarck might regard this treaty as a mere 'stop-gap' – a stepping stone towards an alliance that would embrace Russia.

* The years from 1881 to about 1885/6 were undoubtedly the heyday of the Bismarckian system. Germany's security was guaranteed by her alliances with Austria-Hungary, Russia and Italy. France was not only isolated from the continental powers but also, after 1882, at odds with Britain because of the quarrel over Egypt. Bismarck could exploit the animosities among other powers, creating a 'balancing of discontents' (a situation in which the other states were kept from forming coalitions against Germany by their relations with one another). Berlin was truly the diplomatic centre of Europe.

This happy state of affairs was short-lived. The revival of fierce Austro-Russian antagonism over Bulgaria in 1886–87 revealed the fragility of the Bismarckian system. When the Austrians openly threatened Russia with war in November 1886 if she invaded Bulgaria, the *Dreikaiserbund* of 1881 was in ruins. When both of his allies turned to Germany for support, Bismarck was faced with a grave dilemma. If he rebuffed Russia, she might turn to France, reviving the old nightmare of a Franco-Russian alliance. If he offered Austria-Hungary no support, she might abandon the German alliance and turn to Britain and France, reviving the 'Crimean Coalition' of 1854, in which Germany had no place. Bismarck's solution to the dilemma was ingenious, 'combining the apparently incompatible'. Having conceded Russia's demands in the Reinsurance Treaty of June 1887, he persuaded Britain to support the Austrians in resisting Russia through the Mediterranean Agreement of December 1887.

* The Reinsurance Treaty highlights the problem of evaluating Bismarck's diplomacy. On the one hand, it could be seen as another example of a flexible policy of keeping his options open by ever more resourceful methods. Most historians, however, regard the Reinsurance Treaty as a desperate device to see Germany through an acute crisis – 'an expedient for postponing a war on two fronts', as Taylor calls it. In that case, it was just another stop-gap designed to prevent a breach between Russia and Germany and pre-empt a Franco-Russian alliance.

The fact that Bismarck did not use the Reinsurance Treaty as a basis for a major improvement in Russo-German relations suggests that he himself viewed the treaty as a temporary measure. But he had little to put in its place.

The lack of fresh initiatives made the Bismarckian structure seem rather stale and fragile by the late 1880s. Bismarck himself admitted privately that the Austro-German alliance was weak and that the other alliances with states such as Italy and Serbia did not constitute a bloc. The only way out of the *impasse* was to strengthen Germany's ties with one of the two 'flanking' powers, Russia or Britain. But, after concluding the Reinsurance Treaty in June 1887, Bismarck had deliberately antagonised Russia in November by preventing her from raising loans in Germany. Although he made proposals to Britain for an alliance in early 1889, he seemed unmoved by the British government's non-committal response – unlike the groups who were advocating the creation of an anti-Russian bloc in central Europe with Britain covering the rear.

By the late 1880s, Bismarck seems to have become pessimistic, even fatalistic. He remarked to a general, 'The task of our policy is, if possible, to prevent war and if that is not possible at least to postpone it'. Contemporary opinion in Germany found this policy stultifying – a 'healthy war was preferable to a morbid peace', it was said. Holstein

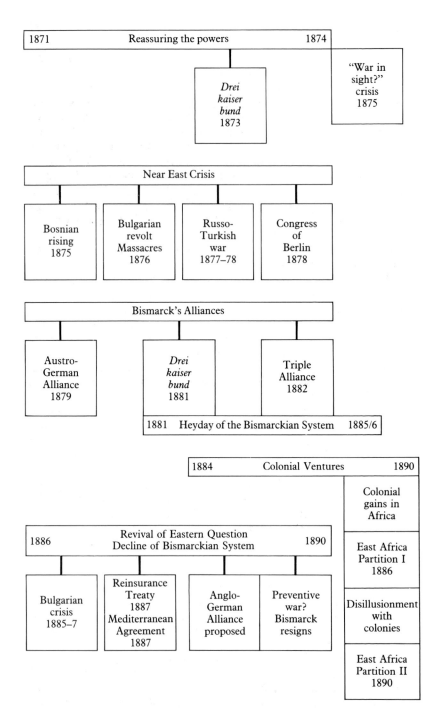

1871	Reassuring the powers	1874

| *Drei kaiser bund* 1873 | "War in sight?" crisis 1875 |

Near East Crisis

| Bosnian rising 1875 | Bulgarian revolt Massacres 1876 | Russo-Turkish war 1877–78 | Congress of Berlin 1878 |

Bismarck's Alliances

| Austro-German Alliance 1879 | *Drei kaiser bund* 1881 | Triple Alliance 1882 |

| 1881 | Heyday of the Bismarckian System | 1885/6 |

| 1884 | Colonial Ventures | 1890 |

Colonial gains in Africa

| 1886 | Revival of Eastern Question Decline of Bismarckian System | 1890 |

East Africa Partition I 1886

| Bulgarian crisis 1885–7 | Reinsurance Treaty 1887 Mediterranean Agreement 1887 | Anglo-German Alliance proposed | Preventive war? Bismarck resigns |

Disillusionment with colonies

East Africa Partition II 1890

Summary – Bismarck and Europe, 1871–90

commented in early 1888: 'Here everyone is for war, with almost the sole exception of Bismarck'. Others demanded the abandonment of Bismarck's European-centred diplomacy for a policy of overseas expansion. His most influential critics insisted that the Reinsurance Treaty, due to expire in 1890, was both contradictory and dangerous. After Bismarck's resignation in 1890, the alliance with Russia was not renewed.

* A century after his fall from power, opinions are still divided about his overall achievements in foreign policy from 1871 to 1890. Bismarck's admirers point out that he steered Germany very skilfully through difficult situations, especially Balkan crises, and made Berlin the centre of international affairs. He achieved his major aim of making Germany secure by neutralising the threat from France and preventing an Austro-Russian conflict, and preserved European peace. If his solutions were only short term ones, they nevertheless worked well enough for two decades, and it was his successors who abandoned his maxim of 'keeping open the wire to St Petersburg'.

Bismarck's critics argue that his success was limited and that his greatest achievements in foreign affairs were accomplished in the decade following 1871. Thereafter he clung rather doggedly to his success in 1881 in 'squaring the circle' of Austro-Russian hostility. Although the fragility of his alliance system was exposed in 1886–87, he produced no constructive alternative, apart from the Reinsurance Treaty. The need to make this treaty has led historians to question whether the so-called 'Bismarckian system' really constituted a system at all. If Bismarck's alliances were a series of stop-gaps, they may only have amounted to a form of 'crisis management' lacking long term aims. Faced with the nightmare of a war on two fronts, Bismarck seems to have planned to abandon Austria-Hungary in order to secure Russian neutrality. If Germany's security rested on such slender foundations then Bismarckian diplomacy was indeed played out by 1890 and his contemporaries were right to see no future in it.

Making notes on 'Bismarck and Europe, 1871–80'

As you read this chapter, give close attention to three aspects: 1 The use of alliances to counter threats to Germany's security; 2 How to assess Bismarck's achievements; 3 The major aspects of the Eastern Question as an issue in European diplomacy. You will be well advised to study the maps carefully to make sure that you do not confuse one place with another – for instance Bosnia with Bulgaria! The following headings and sub-headings should provide a suitable framework for your notes:
1.   Threats to Germany's security. Was Bismarck unduly alarmist?
2.   The Near East crisis. What was Bismarck's role?

Review your notes on aspects of the Eastern Question. Because there are so many events to be covered for this topic, it might be useful to draw up a separate time-chart to show what happened and in what order.

Answering essay questions on '*Bismarck and Europe, 1871–90*'

Most of the questions asked on this topic, as on the other topics covered by this book, require an analytical, as opposed to a descriptive, approach. The trick is to be able to identify the key points in a problem or situation and to construct an argument or discussion around them. The relevant factual knowledge you possess is primarily used as 'evidence' to substantiate the points you are making.

There are a number of key points that are common to most questions that can be asked about Bismarck's foreign policy, 1871–90. If you look back over your note headings, you should be able to see what they are. Those you might have identified are: aims and objectives; policy towards France; Austro-Russian relations and the Balkans; the alliance system; and persuading Britain to oppose Russia. Colonial policy might also be added, for use if it seemed relevant. Essays on Bismarck's foreign policy between 1871 and 1890 will normally include a discussion of some or all of these key points. Questions on the topic tend to focus on one of three issues: the influence of Balkan problems on Bismarckian diplomacy; the success/failure of Bismarck's foreign policy; and the Congress of Berlin's solutions to the Eastern Question. Study the following questions which have been grouped on the basis of these issues:

1 What problems did Bismarck encounter in his attempts to maintain the *Dreikaiserbund*?
2 How far were the lines of Bismarck's foreign policy determined by crises in the Balkans?
3 'His concern was the security of the German Empire; his achievement was the domination of Europe.' Discuss this view of Bismarck's foreign policy.
4 Was Bismarck's foreign policy 1871–90 a success?
5 'Bismarck's greatest triumphs were gained from 1871 to 1890'. Discuss this comment on his foreign policy.
6 Was Bismarck's foreign policy failing by 1890?
7 'At the Congress of Berlin in 1878 the complicated Eastern Question was successfully dealt with by negotiation'. Discuss this statement.
8 Consider the strengths and weaknesses of the settlement reached at the Congress of Berlin (1878).
9 Why did the Eastern Question threaten European peace in the years 1875–78? How far did the Treaty of Berlin provide a satisfactory solution?

Questions 1 and 2 are fairly straightforward. They require a discussion of a central issue in Bismarck's diplomacy – how to avoid an Austro-Russian conflict over the Balkans. It is important to note, however, that they are different types of questions that require a different approach when answering them. Question 1 is a 'direct' question. To answer it, you need four or five main points (or paragraph headings), each one backed up with evidence. A review of your notes under headings 2, 4 and 6 should suggest what these headings could be, providing a basic framework for an answer.

Question 2, one of the 'how far/to what extent?' type of questions, requires an approach which will enable you to argue a case for and against the proposition contained in the question. Under one heading, list the points *for* (Bismarck's foreign policy *was* determined by Balkan crises): under the second heading, list the points *against*. Now re-arrange these points in some sort of order, so that you have about three paragraph points under each heading. Consider the relative strength of the two sides of the argument. This probably shows that the main thrust of the answer will be 'yes' – Balkan crises did largely determine the lines of Bismarck's policy – but with a subsidiary argument about isolating France. In which order would you present the two sides of the argument? The stronger case first, perhaps?

Questions such as number 3 are the 'challenging statement' type. They look more difficult, but they are really a variation of the 'how far' type. Although you could take the statement as a whole and use the *for* and *against* technique, as for question 2, it might be easier to split the question into two parts. In this case you could use as your headings 'security of Germany' and 'domination of Europe' and list three paragraph points under each. You may also want to question whether Bismarck's 'domination of Europe' persisted right up to 1890 but, in general, your two headings do not represent, in this particular question, opposing sides of an argument.

Questions 4–6 are also, in essence, of the 'to what extent' type. You will need to consider how success can be measured (see your note – heading no 7). You could then list points under two headings 'successes' and 'failures'. Which is the stronger argument? Will that influence which aspect you deal with first? You may feel, however, that a crucial point is whether the successes were only short term ones. If so, you may decide that this point should be given some prominence (at least one paragraph) in a discussion of Bismarckian foreign policy.

Similar considerations apply to questions 7–9, even though the subject matter is very different. Question 7 is another 'challenging statement' question, for which you would need to argue a case *for* and *against* the success of the Berlin Congress. Question 8 shows a simple way of doing it! Question 9 is clearly in two parts. The first part is a 'direct' question, requiring a number of points backed by evidence, while the second part calls for the approach used earlier for the 'how far' type of question. Would the two parts of your answer necessarily be of the same length? Identifying the type of question that is being asked is important, because it should help you to see which of several approaches is the most appropriate one for you to use in your essay. It might be worthwhile to go through the list of questions again to see how readily you can identify the various types of questions.

Source-based questions on 'Bismarck and Europe, 1871–90'

1 The Near East Crisis, 1875–78

Read carefully the extracts from the documents written by Bismarck to Bülow (page 21) and by Russell to Derby (page 20). Answer the following questions:

a) Explain the 'incompatibility of . . . interests' referred to in line 4 of the first extract.

b) What is Bismarck's major aim in the Crisis, as suggested in both extracts?

c) What evidence is there that the first extract is from a confidential internal memorandum?

d) In the second extract, Russell is supposedly reporting Bismarck's views. Does Russell consider Bismarck to be genuine? Explain your answer.

e) Which of Bismarck's fears, expressed in either extract, became reality by 1890?

2 Bismarck and the Congress of Berlin, 1878

Read carefully the extracts from the writings of Austrian and Russian diplomats at the Congress of Berlin, given on pages 26–27. Answer the following questions:

a) Who are i) Andrassy, and ii) Beaconsfield?

b) Which country seems to be most displeased with Bismarck? What does this displeasure suggest about the expectations of that country?

c) What personal values does the writer of the first set of extracts display? How do these values affect his attitude towards the various participants in the Congress?

d) Which extracts come closest to identifying Bismarck's motives at the Congress as you understand them? Explain your answer.

e) What appears to be the purpose of the Russian diplomat in writing as he does?

3 Disraeli and the Congress of Berlin, 1878

Examine the *Punch* cartoon reproduced on page 28. Answer the following questions:

a) Which three 'countries' do the characters in the cartoon represent?

b) What does the artist wish you to believe about the part Disraeli played at the Congress of Berlin? Explain your answer.

c) Explain the significance of 'ASIAN FRONTIER' as the name written on the wall.

d) What is the artist's attitude towards i) Turkey, and, ii) Cyprus? Support your answers with evidence.

4 Bismarck and Russia, 1879

Read carefully the extract from the Tsar's letter to the Kaiser, given on page 29. Answer the following questions:

a) Who are i) 'the brave Montenegrins', and ii) 'the European commissioners'?

b) What is the Tsar's complaint?

c) How had the situation changed from that described by the Russian diplomat, on page 27? Why was this?

d) In what ways did the Tsar, in his letter, attempt to exert pressure on the Kaiser?

5 Bismarck and Austria-Hungary, 1887

Read carefully the extract from the Austro-Hungarian foreign minister's
memorandum, given on pages 35–36. Answer the following questions:
a) What criticism is being made of Bismarck?
b) What possible explanation of Bismarck's behaviour is suggested?
c) What was the probable purpose of the document from which the
   extract is taken? Explain your answer.
d) What is the attitude of the author of the document towards
   Bismarck and Germany? Explain your answer.

6 Bismarck and Britain, 1887

Read carefully the extracts from Bismarck's letters, given on pages
36–37. Answer the following questions:
a) What does Bismarck suggest, in the two letters, are the criteria
   he will use when making decisions about foreign policy?
b) What is Bismarck attempting to achieve in his letter to Salisbury?
   Justify your answer.
c) Why did Bismarck regard British participation in the agreement
   with Austria-Hungary and Italy as being important?
d) What is the ostensible purpose of the letter from which the first
   extract is taken? What other purposes are hinted at?
e) Was Bismarck's policy towards Britain a success? Explain your
   answer.

CHAPTER 3

Colonial Rivalries, 1870–1914

1 The Great Powers and Colonies Before 1870

European expansion overseas began long before industrialisation. The great 'Age of Discovery' was the sixteenth century, not the nineteenth. Between 1450 and 1815 Spain and Portugal, followed by Holland, France and Britain, acquired overseas empires in Africa, the Americas, India and South East Asia. Some were colonies of white settlement, such as North America; some were plantation colonies, in which a European élite employed slave labour, such as the West Indian sugar islands; while others were little more than trading bases. During these centuries enterprising European merchants traded all over the globe, not just with colonies.

 * In the early nineteenth century Britain, as the Duke of Wellington observed, 'had possession of nearly every valuable port and colony in the world'. Serious doubts existed, however, whether overseas possessions (India excepted) were anything but 'millstones around our neck' – 'wretched burdens which we assumed in an evil hour'. A British minister asserted, in reference to Africa, that 'dominion over the whole of that vast continent would be but a worthless prize'. In 1865, a Parliamentary Report recommended that Britain should abandon her few possessions in West Africa. The period 1815 to 1870 has therefore been seen by some writers as an age of 'anti-imperialism'.

There was undoubtedly some disillusionment with colonies in mid-nineteenth century Britain. The attitude of colonial settlers towards the mother country was seen as a mixture of ingratitude and a desire for independence. The American colonists, for example, had thrown off their allegiance to Britain in the 1780s while Canadians, among others, contributed little – and that reluctantly – to the costs of their own defence. An observer commented in 1865, 'The normal course of colonial history is the perpetual assertion of the right to self-government'. In response to such demands, European settlers in colonies such as Canada and Cape Colony (South Africa) were granted more control over their own affairs.

Furthermore, by about 1850 the economic justification for colonies, long disputed by some political economists, was wearing thin. The practice of regulating the trade of the colonies to suit the interests of the mother country (known as the 'old colonial system') ceased to have much point. It was noted that Britain did more trade with America after independence than before it. The pattern of Britain's overseas trade was changing and the colonies were no longer Britain's best trading partners. With the gradual abandonment of the regulations of the 'old colonial system' in favour of free trade, colonial trade ceased to have a special role in Britain's expanding world commerce. This expansion of trade was a sign of the industrial supremacy she enjoyed over her European rivals and had little to do with empire.

* Despite this 'anti-imperialist' mood, Britain did not actually give up an existing colony of any significance in the period 1815–1870. Rather the reverse, in fact. Singapore, Aden, Hong Kong and Lagos became British possessions acquired, in the main, as trading stations or naval bases. Australia and New Zealand also became colonies, following a revival of interest in emigration as a palliative to over-population. Neither justification could be used to explain the enormous extension of British rule in India. The Indian Mutiny of 1857 led to some re-thinking about *how* India should be governed, but not to *whether* it should continue to be governed by Britain. India, of course, was always regarded as a special case – 'the jewel of the crown'. Apart from considerations of power and prestige, Britain's trade with India seemed to require a British political presence. An additional factor was that the cost of defending India was met from local revenues, which was not the case with Canada and other imperial possessions. The notion that this was a period of 'anti-imperialism' in Britain therefore needs to be qualified.

The mid-nineteenth century also saw both France and Russia extending their empires. French imperialism was mainly a quest for prestige although it was sometimes encouraged by interest groups such as the Lyons silk industry. Algeria became a colony of settlement in the two decades following the initial conquest in 1830. In the 1860s French control was being asserted over parts of Indo-China. In the previous decade French power in Senegal, in West Africa, was extended under a remarkably dynamic colonial governor. His creation of well-trained African regiments, the Senegalese *tirailleurs* (sharpshooters) laid the base for French military imperialism in West Africa.

The military also played a key role in the 'inexorable advance of Russia across Central Asia' which so alarmed the Government of India because it brought Russian forces to within striking distance of Afghanistan, adjacent to India's north west frontier. The Russian advance began in the 1840s and continued at a faster tempo in the 1860s. The capture of Tashkent and Bokhara put most of Turkestan under Russian control. Further eastwards, Russia secured the cession of territory that made the Tsarist Empire a neighbour of China, obtaining in addition an outlet on the Pacific Ocean, the future Vladivostok. Russian imperialism was essentially land-based, designed to assert Russian prestige and to challenge Britain in Asia, where she could not use her sea-power to much effect. Although much of the expansion was seemingly carried out by 'men on the spot' – ambitious generals and expansionist-minded Governor Generals – the driving force behind it was the war ministry. With the backing of the Tsar, they could ignore the objections of the treasury or the foreign ministry which disliked the financial and diplomatic repercussions of this expansionist move across Asia. In one sense, therefore, there may not have been a coherent official policy of Asiatic expansion. Once begun, the conquest of turbulent peoples on Russia's borders could be almost infinitely extended on the grounds that the really secure frontier always lay further ahead. A similar situation prevailed in India.

The extension of British territorial rule in India through military action was not the typical form of British expansion in this period. It was her overwhelming economic and naval superiority that enabled her to exercise influence well beyond the limits of her 'formal' empire. Such was the case, for example, in Africa and the Persian Gulf and, to some extent, in China. In Latin America, Britain established an economic preponderance reinforced by treaty rights.

* Hence in a supposedly 'anti-imperialist' age, three of the European powers had extended their political and/or economic influence over non-European states or societies. The reasons for this were varied. In some cases it was to assist trade; in others prestige was the main consideration. Frequently, especially where existing frontiers were being pushed forward, the impetus for expansion came from 'the men on the spot', rather than from political leaders in the capitals of Europe. A similar mixture of motives continued to influence European imperialism in the later decades of the century.

2 Africa and the Europeans Before 1870

There have been some important changes in recent years in historians' assessment of the impact of Europe on Africa in the nineteenth century. As knowledge of Africa's rich past has increased, so many earlier assumptions about the nature of African societies have needed to be reconsidered. Thus the traditional view that the Europeans 'shaped a passive Africa to their will' is no longer tenable. Vitality, rather than passivity, seems more appropriate to describe Africa in 1870. Imperialism should therefore be regarded as a process of interaction, in which Europeans and Africans were reacting to changes that were taking place both in Europe and Africa.

This was not how most Victorians saw Africa. To them it was the 'Dark Continent' about which little was known. They assumed that there was little to be known – that Africa had no history, and that the Africans themselves were virtually unchanged since prehistoric times. From this false assumption it was but a short step to an imaginary 'Darkest Africa' sunk in barbarism. Thus the absence of divisions into European-style states or nations was interpreted as a sign that anarchy reigned. The diversity of the peoples of Africa was often neglected in favour of stereotypes. Hence the savagery of some tribes, highlighted by sensationalist travellers' tales, and the laziness of others were regarded as typical of most Africans. 'Darkest Africa' was seemingly inhabited by culturally, if not racially, inferior peoples, devoted to superstitions and pagan rites. At best they were 'children' who needed a firm hand and the Bible to teach them the benefits of civilisation and Christianity. Europeans were seemingly unaware of the spread of the Islamic faith in large parts of Africa.

This ignorance was despite the fact that numerous Europeans in coastal settlements in West Africa mingled and inter-married with Africans. Traders and government officials made treaties with local chiefs. The device of 'protectorates' was based on the assumption that a workable relationship could be created on the basis of mutual trust and even respect. There are therefore some unresolved ambiguities in the Europeans' perception of Africans that are not easy to account for.

In political terms, a number of significant developments took place between 1815 and 1870. In North Africa, French rule was firmly established in Algeria. European influence was also growing in Tunisia and Egypt and, to some extent, in Tripoli. These three states were still under the nominal suzerainty of the Sultan of Turkey. In South Africa, European rule was steadily expanding despite native resistance. The Boers, descendants of the original Dutch settlers, established new settlements outside British control. The Transvaal and Orange Free State were recognised by Britain as independent republics in the 1850s. Although the British government attempted fitfully to protect native interests, its main concern was the Cape. Cape Colony was regarded as a vital base on the route to India – both before and after the opening of the Suez Canal in 1869. In 1872 Cape Colony was granted self-government but this did not mean the end of the British government's involvement in the affairs of South Africa.

In Africa south of the Saraha desert (sub-Saharan), major changes were taking place in tribal power relationships. This is an aspect of what some writers call 'the African partition of Africa'. The term covers a series of complex events such as the *jihads* or holy wars of the Islamic empires in the northerly parts of West Africa and the *mfecane* – the Zulu despotism – in southern Africa. The friendly response of some African tribes to the European presence later in the century was sometimes the result of their experience of these internal wars. To the defeated and displaced tribes, the Europeans might well seem, by comparison, relatively innocuous interlopers, or even potential allies.

* The economic penetration of Africa by Europe began well before the age of imperialism. European goods such as cotton cloth, firearms and spirits, as well as Indian and American textiles, were found in many parts of Africa before 1870. The major economic change taking place after 1815 was the gradual decline of the slave trade. Although many European states had agreed in 1815 to follow Britain's lead in

abolishing the slave trade, in practice there was much evasion for several decades. However, in West Africa where the ban on slaving was enforced by the British navy, a thriving trade in tropical products developed. In addition to palm oil (in demand as a machine lubricant and for soap), vegetable oils, timber, ivory and gum were in great demand in Europe.

From Sierra Leone to the Niger, Britain enjoyed a sort of 'informal empire' on the cheap. Four naval stations and a few consuls were enough for the exercise of British political and economic influence. Apart from trading stations, territorial acquisitions were generally neither wanted nor necessary.

In West-Central Africa (the Congo and Angola) where British naval patrols were few, the slave trade actually expanded for some decades, becoming so profitable that slavers penetrated up to 1000 miles inland. The sudden cessation of the trade in the 1850s, when Portugal at last prohibited the trade to Brazil, disrupted the economy of the region.

East Africa's commercial links were with Arabia and India, not Europe. The island of Zanzibar became the centre of a thriving trade in ivory, gum and cloves as well as slaves, despite British attempts to persuade the Sultan of Zanzibar to abolish the slave trade. Some European merchants were also attempting to create trading ventures in the region.

The Sahara desert acted as a great divide. The states of North Africa were much more closely integrated into the economy of Europe and the Near East than was most of sub-Saharan Africa. The size of the European commercial communities in these states was growing, quite rapidly in the case of Egypt. In both Tunisia and Egypt excessive borrowing had created a massive foreign debt by 1870. The former was subjected to an International Debt Commission in 1868 and the thirtyfold increase in the Egyptian debt between 1863 and 1876 made the country vulnerable to even greater European influence.

In the course of the period 1815 to 1870, therefore, the commercial links between Europe and most regions of Africa were growing stronger with each decade. Africa's trade expanded and she became more closely integrated into the international economy. In other respects, however, the gap between Africa and Europe was widening. World trade was expanding at a much faster rate than the African economy as a whole. Nor was it, of course, just a question of disparity in economic growth. Despite the vitality of African life, the encounter between Africans and Europeans after 1870 did not take place on equal terms. The rapid technological advance of the leading European states, expressed partly in the form of steamships and railways and partly in the shape of more deadly weapons of war, meant that a major imbalance of power existed between Europeans and Africans by about 1870.

3 Colonial Rivalry and the Partition of Africa

The partition of Africa amongst the great powers was accomplished in about twenty years, roughly between 1880 and 1900. Equally striking was the sheer scale of the share-out. By 1900, only about one tenth of Africa had not fallen under European rule, whereas twenty years earlier only one tenth had been colonised. To the existing colonial powers of Britain, France, Spain and Portugal were now added Germany, Italy and Belgium. From a European perspective, the partition of Africa resembled a headlong rush to acquire colonial possessions. Hence the phrase the 'Scramble' for Africa. From an African perspective, on the other hand, it was a gradual process extending over a lengthy period. European rule did not immediately make much impression on native societies in the interior of Africa. As late as 1905, only a small minority of Africans had seen a white face. Life went on as usual for some years after the signing of treaties with Europeans.

In effect, there were two stages to the partition. Firstly, the powers staked out a claim to territory and lines were drawn on a map of Africa, usually without much relevance to the realities of tribal relationships. This stage often amounted to little more than a 'paper partition'. Then, during the 1890s, the serious business of conquest and consolidation began. Even then, most colonial governments were weak. In both conquest and consolidation, the Europeans were often dependent on the co-operation and assistance of friendly tribes. The European powers usually preferred to proclaim protectorates over African territories rather than to formally annex them. African chiefs were persuaded to sign treaties with European officials or commercial agents which, initially, granted some rather vague jurisdiction or influence to Europeans. This laid the basis for what came to be known as 'indirect rule'. In some cases, European governments granted very wide powers to Chartered Companies to exercise administrative authority as well as conducting commercial operations. This was empire 'on the cheap', and indicates how reluctant governments were to take on the expense of creating a proper colonial administration.

* The years 1879 to 1886 were a time of extensive colonial rivalry amongst the European powers in Africa. The Scramble was on! In Egypt, West Africa, the Congo, southern Africa and East Africa, the powers asserted claims to political influence or territorial control. A feature of the Scramble was that Britain was involved in rivalry with virtually every other European power at one stage or another. There was also an anti-British element to it. This is not surprising since Britain had used her sea-power to assert a sort of 'paramountcy' over most of Africa's coasts in the mid-nineteenth century. One of the few rivalries in which Britain was not directly involved was the assertion of a French protectorate over Tunisia in 1881–82, which angered the

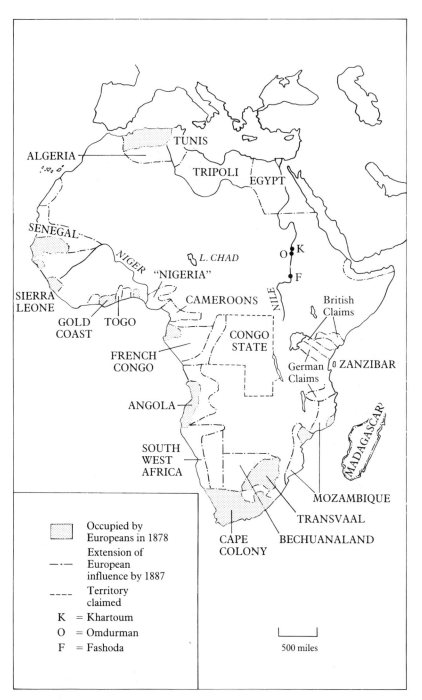

The partition of Africa: European rule, 1878 and 1887

Italians, whose nationals greatly outnumbered French residents in the area. Egyptian nationalists were also alarmed by France's action, fearing a similar fate would befall their country.

* A joint Franco-British supervision of Egypt's finances had been set up following a declaration of bankruptcy in 1878. When the ruler, the Khedive, was deposed for intriguing against the Dual Control of France and Britain, resentment against foreign interference rapidly increased. A nationalist movement, led by an army officer, Arabi Pasha, seemed to threaten the Dual Control. In Britain, the 'anti-imperialist' Liberal government under Gladstone vacillated and was partly pushed and partly drifted into a confrontation with Arabi Pasha. Anti-foreign riots and the British bombardment of Alexandria in July 1882 escalated the crisis so that the safety of the Suez Canal was thought to be at risk. The British government, deserted by France at a critical moment, despatched an expeditionary force which defeated Arabi Pasha's army in September 1882. Since evacuation seemed impossible, given the political chaos then existing, Britain remained in occupation of Egypt to restore stability. Thus began a temporary occupation that lasted for 40 years!

Egypt became a contentious issue between France and Britain because Gladstone decided not to revive the Anglo-French partnership. This was a severe blow to French pride because of France's historic and cultural ties with Egypt. Another reason for French pique was, as a French historian put it, 'The French found it difficult to forgive the British for not having shared their indecisiveness' during the crisis in the summer of 1882.

French sensitivities would only have been satisfied by a British withdrawal from Egypt but this was made less likely by a revolt in the Egyptian Sudan. The Egyptian army was defeated by the rebel forces while the cost of the military operations destroyed the state's precarious finances, which now needed an international loan to restore solvency. Supervision of the country's financial administration was subsequently placed in the hands of an international commission, on which the French and Russian delegates opposed British proposals. Consequently, in order to be able to govern Egypt, Britain needed German support on the debt commission. Thus, until the financial position of the Egyptian government became much stronger, Bismarck was able to pursue a policy of benign blackmail – the 'Egyptian lever' as it was called. The price for Germany's support was colonial concessions in Africa and elsewhere. The difficulties this created for Britain were summed up by Salisbury in this despatch of 23 February 1887.

1 We are steering in very narrow channels and we are in constant danger of running aground on one side or the other. On the one hand, English opinion is not prepared for an evacuation of Egypt

still less for the abandonment of it. . . . On the other hand, we
5 must kept it diplomatically in our power to satisfy France on
account of Bismarck's attitude. His policy in a humbler walk of
life would be called *chantage* (blackmail). He is perpetually telling
us of the offers France is making of reconciliation on the basis
of an attack upon England in Egypt, and of the sacrifices which
10 Germany makes by refusing these proposals; sacrifices for which,
he adds, England must make some return, and then he demands
this and that. I heartily wish we had never gone into Egypt.
Had we not done so, we could snap our fingers at all the world.

* In West Africa, French activity greatly increased in the late 1870s
and early 1880s. This provoked Britain into asserting a protectorate
over areas where she had previously exerted only an informal influence.
A good example of this is the Niger delta, where British companies
had been trading for decades. The intrusion of two French trading
companies in the 1880s and the appearance of French warships along
the coast signalled the intensification of Anglo-French rivalry. In
response to this challenge, Britain engaged in treaty-making with local
chiefs. These treaties enabled the British government to declare a
formal protectorate over the Niger region in 1885.

Another development which contributed to the Scramble was the
revival of ambitious schemes for French expansion into what was
called the Western Soudan. This was to be achieved through the
creation of a railway network that would link Senegal, Algeria and
the Upper Niger. The railways, it was believed, would develop a trade
estimated at 100 million francs a year. The reality was more prosaic.
After 20 years, the export trade of this new 'Eldorado' amounted to
a mere 3 million francs a year. The railway scheme was mostly
abandoned but it nevertheless gave the green light to the French
imperialist groups in Senegal. The eventual creation of a vast French
empire in West Africa in the 1880s and 1890s was largely the
achievement of the French colonial army, frequently acting contrary
to instructions from Paris.

* Important as were the Niger and the Nile in terms of
Anglo-French rivalry, it was the Congo that fully highlighted the
competitiveness of the so-called 'New Imperialism' of the 1880s.
Leopold, King of the Belgians, intended to exploit the economic
potential of the Congo (ivory and rubber) for personal financial gain.
He set up an International Association in 1877 to open up the region,
which attracted widespread support in Europe. Thus began what
appears to have been one of the most remarkable 'confidence tricks'
of the age – the projection of a profit-making scheme as a scientific
and humanitarian endeavour. The International Association had been
actively concluding treaties with African chiefs in the Congo. Although
they were clearly commercial in nature, they were later claimed to

have transferred sovereignty over the region to the Association. This provoked France into making rival claims.

The British government tried to counter French claims by concluding a treaty with Portugal, recognising her ancient, if shadowy, claims to jurisdiction in the area. France and Germany, however, objected to this 'private arrangement' to exclude their activities. Consequently the question was submitted to an international conference, which took place at Berlin from November 1884 to February 1885.

The Berlin Conference gave formal recognition to European claims to territory in Africa and laid down the 'ground rules' for the partition over the next few years. The Congo Free State was recognised as a sovereign state with guarantees of freedom of commerce to all nations. The doctrine of 'effective occupation' laid down at the conference was intended to put a stop to Britain's practice of asserting a vague right to 'influence' over many parts of Africa. It thereby obliged the powers to define their claims with some precision and reinforce them with tangible signs of their presence. Hence the resort to the device of the Chartered Company to avoid the expense of a colonial administration. At the Berlin Conference, Germany also formalised her claims to Togo and the Cameroons, German East Africa and South West Africa.

* German involvement in African affairs was a new factor in the 1880s – and an important aspect of the so-called 'New Imperialism' of this period. Colonial issues offered a unique opportunity for Franco-German co-operation – directed against Britain. Bismarck's proposal in 1884 for a Franco-German front struck a responsive chord with Jules Ferry, the French premier at that time and an ardent colonialist. Revenge for her exclusion from Egypt could be combined with the assertion of French claims in West Africa and the Congo. Bismarck also had a grievance against Britain in South West Africa which led him to retaliate against what he regarded as British arrogance towards German interests there. Angered by the endless delays in his negotiations with Britain, Bismarck decided in August 1884 to defend the interests of a German trading company by asserting a claim to South West Africa. The significance of this move was that southern Africa, hitherto an almost exclusively British preserve, became involved in great power rivalries.

In 1886, the economic and political situation in southern Africa was revolutionised by the discovery of gold in the Transvaal. From being a poor pastoral farming community, the Transvaal became potentially the wealthiest state in southern Africa and a threat to British imperial interests. This was because the growing economic power of the Transvaal not only put the dominance of Cape Colony at risk, but also threatened to weaken the loyalty of the Cape Boers to British rule. How then were imperial interests in southern Africa to be defended?

One answer was to establish a British presence in Rhodesia to act as a counterweight to the Boer republic of the Transvaal. This was the solution offered by Cecil Rhodes. 'If we get Mashonaland – (Rhodesia)', he said, 'we shall get the balance of Africa'. Rhodes, an Englishman who had made a fortune out of diamond mining, was an influential figure in Cape politics. In October 1889, he persuaded the British government to grant a royal charter to his British South Africa Company to administer Rhodesia. In this way the threat to imperial interests was checked – at no cost to the Treasury. Under Rhodes' guidance, Rhodesia would strengthen the British element in southern Africa.

Britain and Germany were also rivals in East Africa in the 1880s. To further German interests in the territories of the Sultan of Zanzibar (see map p. 55), Bismarck exploited the 'Egyptian lever', as this report of a conversation between the British ambassador (Sir Edward Malet) and Count Bismarck (Bismarck's son) in October 1886 illustrates:

1 Count Bismarck spoke to me at length today by order of the Chancellor on the subject. He said that the traditional policy of Germany and the one which was most agreeable was to be on the most friendly terms with England, that it had been a matter
5 of deep pain and regret to Prince Bismarck to be obliged to depart from this traditional policy two years ago, in consequence of the way in which he had been treated by England in regard to the colonial policy of Germany . . .

He reverted to the subject now because he once more asked
10 for the assistance and friendly action of the British Government in the matter of Zanzibar. In return for that he would reject all the overtures which might be made to him by the new French ambassador to help France in embarrassing us in Egypt and in all questions in which our interests and those of France were in
15 divergence, he would not only refuse to go against us but would give us such assistance as might be possible consistently with the necessities of his home position. . .

He concluded by pressing on me again the great importance which Prince Bismarck attached to the question and the intimate
20 relation which it bore to the general question of the relations between England and Germany.

A German protectorate was proclaimed over German East Africa (later Tanganyika) in 1885. British commercial interests now redoubled their efforts to secure government backing. This resulted in a partition agreement in 1886, which recognised Germany's stronger claims. Continuing rivalry, involving the risk of serious clashes between British and German groups, made a further partition treaty necessary

WOOING THE AFRICAN VENUS.
(*Some way after Homer's Hymn to Aphrodite.*)

in 1890. This second agreement, known as the Heligoland-Zanzibar Treaty, was much to Britain's advantage and included a protectorate over the dominions of the Sultan of Zanzibar.

* The 1890s saw a new intensity to Anglo-French rivalries, especially in West Africa and the Nile valley. In addition Italy was also making a bid for territory in East Africa, especially in the area known as the

Horn, including Ethiopia and Eritrea. By 1891, the British government was regretting its earlier acceptance of Italian claims along the Red Sea, when they extended their claims to the eastern Sudan. By 1896, however, the Italians were in serious difficulties. When they were defeated by the Ethiopians at the battle of Adowa, their hopes of creating a large Italian empire in East Africa were dashed.

European diplomatic considerations now came into play. The German government feared for the survival of the Italian monarchy and regime if it suffered a further setback to its colonial aspirations. Britain was therefore pressed to intervene. In 1896 a force under General Kitchener was sent from Egypt to the Sudan, to take the pressure off the Italian forces threatened by the Dervishes. In 1898, Kitchener advanced southwards and, having defeated the Dervishes in a great battle at Omdurman, re-occupied Khartoum. By this time a small French force under Captain Marchand had finally reached Fashoda, on the Upper Nile, 400 miles further south. The aim of Marchand's expedition was to reinforce France's demand for an international conference on Egypt and the Sudan which, they believed, would require Britain to evacuate Egypt. This was a dangerous game for France to play.

The British government responded by demanding the unconditional withdrawal of Marchand's expedition. The government in Paris was sensitive to clamour to defend France's honour. The British Cabinet vetoed concessions to France. It was this refusal to compromise that made the confrontation at Fashoda a possible prelude to war between the two countries. The French government, conscious of Britain's overwhelming naval superiority in the late 1890s, eventually climbed down. In November 1898 Marchand was ordered to withdraw from Fashoda.

In the 1890s Anglo-French rivalry in West Africa had also turned into confrontation. The French seemed to be on the move throughout West Africa. French expansion to the east and south east from Senegal clashed with British expansion northwards to preserve the so-called 'hinterlands' of her coastal possessions. A race developed to establish a claim to these disputed regions. A clash between over-zealous commanders of rival forces was always possible, almost creating a state of 'suspended war' in the 1890s. Although governments in Paris and London had no desire for conflict over West Africa they were under considerable pressure to defend national honour and national interests, delaying a final settlement until 1898.

⋆ Southern Africa also presented a problem for the British government in the 1890s. The worsening relations between Britain and the Transvaal made it necessary to ensure that Germany did not support the Boers. Germany's goodwill was secured in 1898 by an agreement on the future division of Portugal's colonies in Africa. Portugal's severe financial difficulties, amongst other things, made it

QUIT!—PRO QUO?

J. B. "GO AWAY! GO AWAY!!"
FRENCH ORGAN GRINDER. "EH? WHAT YOU GIVE ME IF I GO?"
J. B. "I'LL GIVE YOU SOMETHING IF YOU DON'T!!"

seem likely that she would have to relinquish Angola and Mozambique. Germany's share of the spoils would represent a step towards realising her idea of a Central African empire, while the main advantage for Britain was that Germany officially renounced any concern in the affairs of the Transvaal.

The Boer War (1899–1902) destroyed the mood of 'jingo imperialism' in Britain. The continental press rejoiced at every setback to British arms, revealing how unpopular Britain, the leading imperial power in the world, had become. Her European rivals even discussed schemes for a 'Continental League' directed against her but British seapower acted as a powerful deterrent to such projects.

In the period 1900–1914 Africa ceased to be an object of serious rivalry amongst the great powers. The main exception was North Africa, but even here the rivalry took a different form from that of previous decades. Germany twice challenged France's position in Morocco (in 1905 and 1911) but it was not for the sake of territorial designs on Morocco itself (see pp. 99 and 108). Italy's attempt to seize Tripoli (Libya) in 1911 led to a conflict with Turkey, but the other powers did not become involved in it, because they did not want Turkey to be weakened any further.

It is clear that a striking feature of the Scramble for Africa was the assertion of European political influence or control over vast tracts of African territory, regardless of its current profitability. In China, on the other hand, a genuine 'economic imperialism' can be observed in this same period. This took the form of exercising pressure on the Chinese government to open up the country to more western trade and investment.

4 Great Power Rivalries in China

For a decade after 1895, the Far East became the main focus of international rivalry. Britain's dominant position in trade with China, that stretched back over half a century, was being challenged by other European states. As the economic competition intensified, the rivalry developed political overtones. The 'Far Eastern Crisis', as some writers call it, began with China's defeat by Japan in 1895 and ended with Japan's victory over Russia in 1905. The revelation of China's weakness in 1895 led to a short-lived 'scramble for concessions' by the great powers. This was followed by territorial demands. China seemed to be in danger of being partitioned amongst the powers. But the fact that only two of the powers, Russia and Japan, had serious designs on Chinese territory is an important reason why China avoided Africa's fate. During this decade of crisis, Britain attempted to set limits to the growth of Russian influence over China and signed an alliance with Japan in 1902, after Germany had made plain her unwillingness to

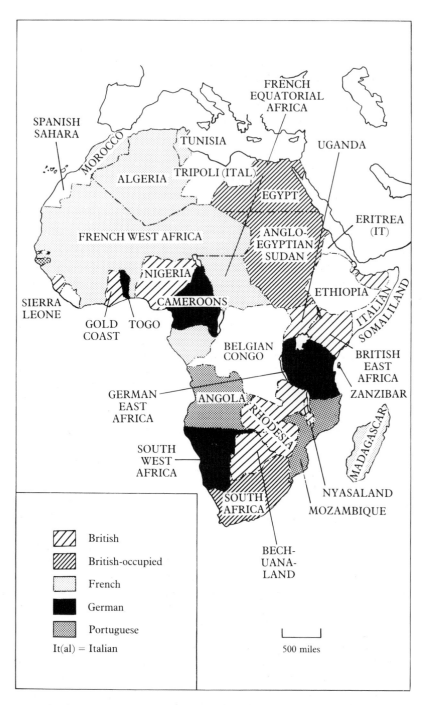

Africa partitioned – 1914

restrain Russia. The Russo-Japanese war of 1904–5 ended the decade of rivalry and tension amongst the powers in the Far East.

* The main interest of Britain, France and Germany in China was economic. Certainly, from a geographical viewpoint, they had no strategic interest in this distant part of the world. Yet although it seems clear that trade and investment were the dominant motives for the western powers' involvement in Chinese affairs, the trade statistics do not seem to justify all the trouble and effort involved in opening up China to western penetration. The explanation is that it was China's potential as a market for manufactured goods (with a population of over 400 million) that made them persevere. As late as 1898, a British minister described China as 'the most hopeful place of the future for the commerce of our country'. But even though Britain had about 70% of China's trade, the reality was that her dealings with China represented about 3% of her total trade in 1885.

* On the other hand, in the 1880s China did seem to offer good investment opportunities for European capital. To western eyes, China was 'ripe' for modernisation. As late as 1880 she had no railways and few modern industries or public utilities, such as gas or water companies. Western business firms and banking interests therefore became engaged in a battle for contracts and 'concessions' for mining rights or railway construction. This commercial competition gave a political dimension to the rivalry of the powers because success in securing economic concessions was seen as a reflection of the political influence that each power exerted in Peking. This is shown by the comment made by a British minister in 1898 about a tussle over a railway concessions: 'We are really fighting a battle for prestige rather than for material gain'.

In the case of Russia and Japan, however, political considerations went far beyond mere prestige. Although the main objective of the Russians was to establish an economic preponderance in Manchuria to assist Russia's industrial development, its realisation depended on establishing political control over this northerly province of China. Japan's response to western imperialism had been to embark on a policy of modernisation, which recognised the need for changes in Japanese society in order to take advantage of western ideas and technology. By the 1890s she possessed a modern navy and a reorganised army. In 1894 she felt strong enough to back her claims over Korea, a Chinese dependency, by force. She rapidly secured control of the sea between Korea and north China and occupied parts of mainland China as well as Korea.

The sudden and unexpected defeat of China by Japan in the war of 1894–95, however, transformed the situation in the Far East. The war demonstrated that Japan was a force to be reckoned with. In fact the Russians were so alarmed at Japan's territorial gains in southern Manchuria, on which Russia herself had designs, that they insisted

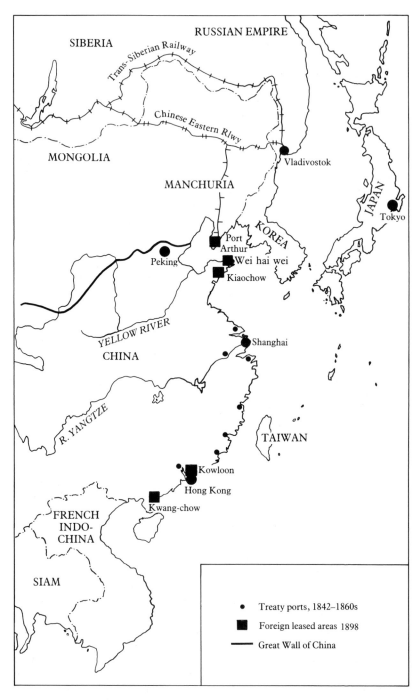

The great powers, Japan and China in the late nineteenth century

on a moderation of Japan's demands in the peace treaty. Japan was thus obliged to return some territory to China, in exchange for a larger financial indemnity. Russia's plan was to create a 'special relationship' with China by posing as her friend and saviour against the Japanese. In return for a large loan, Russia obtained valuable economic concessions in Manchuria. This strategy was essentially a long term one, dependent on the completion of the Trans-Siberian Railway, begun in 1891.

The Sino-Japanese war of 1894–95 had not only revealed China's weakness but also made her heavily dependent (almost for the first time) on foreign loans. The result was a 'scramble for concessions', which, at times, bordered on the absurd. By the time this 'midsummer madness' had abated in 1898, Britain, for example, had acquired concessions to build 2800 miles of railways of which only a few hundred miles had been constructed by 1907! But it also had its more serious side. Russia secured important privileges which included the right to build a railway across Manchuria, greatly reducing the distance from Siberia to Vladivostok. The other powers also obtained railway and mining concessions in various regions of China. Each nation seemed to be carving out a 'sphere of interest', a trend accentuated by the move towards demanding exclusive privileges for that nation in its sphere. While Russia was attempting to dominate northern China, especially Manchuria, France was most active in the south, adjacent to her empire in Indo-China. Meanwhile Britain, traditionally the advocate of the so-called 'Open Door' policy, was seeking to preserve her long-established position in central China, especially the Yangtze basin. Her most serious competitor here was Germany, whose main area of activity was Shantung province in the north-east. By 1898, therefore, the partition of China into spheres of economic interest seemed to be imminent.

* How did China avoid Africa's fate of being partitioned? One factor was that China was a unitary state with a dynasty and a sense of nationhood that Africa lacked. The Chinese authorities also attempted to weaken the trend towards 'spheres' by granting concessions that cut across them. Another factor was the treaty port system in China. By the 1890s, Europeans could trade at over 30 treaty ports and also enjoyed reasonable access to the interior. In short, political control was not necessary for the sake of trade. From the European point of view there were two other considerations that operated against partition. Firstly the realisation dawned that they might lose more than they gained from it. The fact was that there were only two 'plums' (Manchuria and the Yangtze) to be shared amongst four powers. The second consideration was the British government's refusal to yield to the clamour of British mercantile interests to create an exclusively British zone in central China because, as was said, 'We are not prepared to undertake the immense

responsibility of governing what is practically a third of China'. India was more than enough of a headache without adding to such burdens. The British government, therefore, encouraged by an American declaration in favour of the 'Open Door' policy, began successful negotiations with her western rivals to give up demands for exclusive rights in their spheres of interest. With Russia, who refused to give up her privileges in Manchuria, the best the British could do was to secure an agreement in 1899 that eased tension but accepted the spheres concept for railway construction.

In 1900 the Boxer rebellion (organised by the Society of the Harmonious Fists) broke out. Anti-foreigner agitation and riots, including attacks on Europeans and their property, swept through north-eastern China. The most dramatic event was the seven week siege of the foreign legations, or embassies, in Peking. European rivalry was almost forgotten – temporarily. An international force advanced cautiously on the capital and relieved the legations in August 1900. In reprisal for Boxer atrocities, Peking was subjected to an orgy of rape and pillage and punitive expeditions were sent to various parts of north China.

In the course of the Boxer rebellion, much damage was done to the railway system in Manchuria. In retaliation the Russian government decided to tighten its grip on the province. Large numbers of troops were employed in suppressing Boxers and 'bandits'. In early 1901 it was learned that Russia had obtained virtual political, as well as economic, control over Manchuria. It seemed only a matter of time before Russia would be able to dominate Peking. One way to prevent this was to enlist German support, as Chamberlain, the colonial secretary, suggested in September 1900:

1   I am personally unable to believe in the reform of the Chinese
    Empire as a whole or in the permanent maintenance of its
    territorial integrity. Unless Russia breaks up from internal
    difficulties, of which there is no present sign, I believe she will
5   ultimately secure Northern China, and that the 'Open Door' will
    be a mere name so far as this part of the Chinese Empire is
    concerned. It is certain that we are not strong enough by
    ourselves to prevent her from accomplishing such an annexation,
    and both in China and elsewhere it is in our interest that
10 Germany should throw herself across the path of Russia. . . .
    The clash of German and Russian interests, whether in China
    or Asia Minor, would be a guarantee for our safety.
      I think then our policy clearly is to encourage good relations
    between ourselves and Germany, as well as between ourselves
15 and Japan and the United States. . . We should, without urging
    it, let it be known that we shall put no obstacle in the way of
    German expansion in Shantung, nor in the way of the gratification

of Japan's ambition in Korea. But, in return, we should obtain
20 written assurances recognising our claim to predominant interest
and influence in the Yang-Tse Valley. We are not likely ever to
want to take possession of any territory in the interior ourselves;
but we ought to try for some understanding which will keep off
all others, and make it easy to maintain the 'Open Door' in at
least this, the most important portion of the Chinese Empire. . .

When the Germans signed an Agreement on China in October 1900,
the British government wrongly believed that Germany had committed
herself to help to defend the status quo throughout China, as the
terms of the treaty seemed to imply:

1 Her Britannic Majesty's Government and the Imperial German
Government. . . have agreed to observe the following principles
in regard to their mutual policy in China:-
1. It is a matter of joint and permanent international interest
5 that the ports on the rivers and littoral of China should remain
free and open to trade. . . for the nationals of all countries
without distinction; and the two governments agree. . . to uphold
the same for all Chinese territory as far as they can exercise
influence.
10 2. (The two governments) will. . . direct their policy towards
maintaining undiminished the territorial condition of the Chinese
Empire.
3. In case of another Power making use of the complications in
China in order to obtain under any form whatever such territorial
15 advantages, the two Contracting Parties reserve to themselves to
come to a preliminary understanding as to the eventual steps to
be taken for the protection of their own interests in China.
4. The two Governments will communicate this Agreement to
the other Powers. . . and will invite them to accept the principles
20 recorded in it.
AGREEMENT between Germany and Great Britain relative to
China. 16 October, 1900.

* But British expectations of German support were dashed in March
1901 when Germany made plain her 'absolute indifference' to the fate
of Manchuria which, she claimed, was outside the scope of the
agreement. Japan was more forthcoming, because Russia still refused
to concede to her the same predominance in Korea that Russia was
now establishing in Manchuria. The Anglo-Japanese Alliance, signed
in 1902, recognised Japan's special interests in Korea while supporting
the integrity of China. The allies agreed to aid each other if one of
them was attacked by two or more powers. Strengthened by this
assurance of support against a Franco-Russian combination, Japan
was able to take a firm line in her negotiations with Russia. When

these proved inconclusive, Japan launched a surprise attack against Russian forces in the Far East in February 1904. The war ended in 1905 after sweeping Japanese victories both on land and at sea.

The Russo-Japanese war brought to an end the possibility of Russian domination of northern China. The main threat to China's political independence was thereby removed and her territorial integrity ceased to be an issue of great concern to the great powers. For the European powers, therefore, the Far East ceased to be a source of serious tension.

* The activities of the powers in China provide a useful illustration of at least two aspects of imperialism. Firstly, the growing competitiveness for economic advantages turned into a form of political rivalry. Western imperialism in China consequently gave the appearance of being a battle for prestige rather than tangible economic benefits. Secondly, and somewhat paradoxically, the main interest of the European powers (with the possible exception of Russia) remained nevertheless the exploitation of the commercial and financial opportunities that China offered. In contrast to Africa, where the European states acquired vast tracts of territory, the activities of the western powers in the Far East can best be described as 'economic imperialism'.

5 Explanations of Imperialism

An English radical, J A Hobson, writing in 1902, asserted that imperialism was nothing less than a conspiracy promoted by financiers for their own enrichment at the nation's expense. That Hobson should suspect that sinister forces lay behind the annexation of tropical lands is understandable. As he noted, the volume of trade between Britain and these new colonies was small and its profits low. By contrast, Britain's capital investments overseas had greatly increased since 1870. Hobson drew this conclusion:

1 Now we cannot fail to recognise that in dealing with these
  foreign investments we are facing by far the most important
  factor in the economics of Imperialism. . . . The statistics of
  foreign investments shed clear light upon the economic forces
5 which are dominating our policy. While the manufacturing and
  trading classes make little out of their new markets. . . it is quite
  otherwise with the investor. It is not too much to say that the
  modern foreign policy of Great Britain is primarily a struggle
  for profitable markets for investment.

Hobson's emphasis on 'surplus capital' is no longer convincing. The statistics now available show clearly that only a very small proportion of the total was invested in these new colonies. Most of it went to the Americas, Australia or old colonies such as India. Hobson was therefore in error in believing that a causal link existed between the acquisition of new colonies and the large increase in overseas investment.

'Economic imperialism', however, is by no means dead. In recent years historians such as Platt and Hynes have re-stated the importance of trade as an influence on Britain's imperial policy. In general terms, trading conditions undoubtedly became increasingly competitive in the late nineteenth century.

Industrialisation in Germany and France led to an increase in the output of manufactured goods, while the so-called 'Great Depression' of 1873–96 signified a fall in demand for such products. Hence the phrase 'surplus manufactures'. The search for markets for manufactures became increasingly competitive as a consequence. In the 1880s, chambers of commerce in Britain were talking in terms of a 'crisis of over-production'. The problem for British manufacturers was aggravated by Germany and France adopting protective tariffs, while Britain clung to Free Trade. Consequently, not only the British domestic market but also her colonial markets were open to her rivals, who proceeded to introduce some form of discriminatory duties against British goods in their colonies. In the 1890s, when French tariffs were greatly increased, British merchants warned the government that 'Free Trade abroad and prosperity at home were inextricably bound up with imperial expansion'. With her rivals resorting to tariffs in Africa and exclusive concessions in China, it was becoming very difficult to maintain the 'fair field and no favour' which, Platt argues, had been the maxim of British policy since about 1850.

* Both Platt and Hynes see a causal link, in Britain's case, between imperialism and the search for markets for 'surplus manufactures'. Lenin, on the other hand, writing in 1916–17, linked imperialism with the search for raw materials:

1 The principal feature of modern capitalism is the domination of
  monopolistic combines of the big capitalists. These monopolies
  are most firmly established when all the sources of raw material
  are controlled by the one group. . . . Colonial possession alone
5 gives complete guarantee of success to the monopolies against
  all the risk of the struggle with competitors . . . The more
  capitalism is developed, the more the need for raw materials is
  felt, the more bitter competition becomes, and the more feverishly
  the hunt for raw materials proceeds throughout the whole world,
10 the more desperate becomes the struggle for the acquisition of
  colonies.

The emphasis Lenin placed on monopoly is important to his view of imperialism, which he equated with the latest stage of capitalism. He also linked monopoly with 'finance capitalism' – the dominance of banks over manufacturing industry. Like Hobson, he saw investment as more important than trade as a motive for imperialism.

Non-Marxist historians have questioned Lenin's assertions about the nature of capitalism and their appropriateness to colonial powers such as France and Britain, not to mention industrially backward states like Russia and Italy. Even more fundamentally, Lenin's interpretation of imperalism is flawed on the grounds of chronology and logic. Lenin clearly dates the emergence of 'monopoly finance capitalism' at about 1900. Since he asserts that this was the motive force behind imperialism, it cannot logically be used to explain colonial acquisitions made before that date – as most of them were! This does not, of course, invalidate all Marxist interpretations of imperialism. Rosa Luxemburg, for example, one of Lenin's contemporaries, regarded imperialism as the political expression of capitalism at all stages of its development. Capitalism, in her view 'ransacks the whole world, seizing the means of production, if necessary, by force'. Modern Marxist historians, such as Kemp, continue to believe (despite the lack of evidence) that imperialism stemmed from the 'imperative necessities of advanced capitalism'.

* In the late nineteenth century, European commercial and financial interests were active throughout the world – in the Far East, Latin America, North America, the Near East and Africa. In China, most of the great powers were content with pursuing 'economic imperialism' – opening up China to European trade and investment. China was not partitioned, unlike Africa. But many, if not most, European colonies in Africa turned out to be 'white elephants' – an economic liability – during this period. This has naturally made historians question whether 'economic imperialism' has much relevance to the partition of Africa.

The statistical evidence shows clearly that Europe's trade with, and investment in, Africa represented a very small proportion of its worldwide total. Hobson undoubtedly exaggerated the importance of 'surplus capital' as a motive for annexing parts of tropical Africa. For example, British investment in West Africa in 1914 only amounted to about £37 million as against £1780 million in Canada, Australasia and India. Hobson also failed to see the importance of tropical products such as palm oil to Britain. In other words, there is quite a good case to be made that British policy in Africa was influenced by the desire to defend British trade. This might well involve annexing some areas, which Salisbury justified on the grounds that 'we only desire territory because we desire commercial freedom'. It was partly in order to create a tariff regime in her colonies to protect French exports from British competition that made France seek to establish a political influence over parts of West Africa. The fear was therefore quite strong in Britain that her goods would be shut out of potential markets in French or German colonies. This view was expressed quite explicitly by a British official: 'We are forced to extend our direct political influence over a large part of Africa to secure a fair field and no favour for our commerce'. Pressure from German merchants was also one factor that explains Bismarck's sudden interest in Africa in the mid-1880s. By 1890, however, political considerations were foremost as shown by his remark 'my map of Africa lies in Europe'.

* Since European imperialism took different forms in different parts of the world, many modern historians are sceptical about the usefulness of a universal economic theory of imperialism. In the last 20 years much emphasis has been given to political factors as the key to European expansion. Increasing attention is also being paid to the 'peripheral' situation – the role of the non-European societies themselves.

Colonial rivalries can quite legitimately be regarded as a transference on to a world stage of the great power rivalries that had mostly been confined to Europe and the Near East from 1815 to 1870. This is what A J P Taylor calls the 'export of tensions'. It was obviously safer to play out these rivalries in distant lands than in Europe itself. The traditional concept of the balance of power also seems to have been carried over into the age of imperialism. A contemporary observer remarked that 'the great powers are dividing up the continent of Africa. . . in the same manner that they would partition countries such as Poland'. The well-established system of conference diplomacy was also applied to the new rivalries in Africa in the form of the Berlin West Africa Conference of 1884–85. As Baumgart points out, this rivalry had become by the 1880s a pluralistic and universal rivalry, no longer confined to Britain and France in Africa and Asia. There were now many more imperial powers who were competing with each other throughout the world. Contemporaries were very conscious of the competition. Jules Ferry likened it to 'a steeplechase moving headlong towards an unknown destination, accelerating as if propelled by its own speed'. This competitiveness encouraged the tendency towards 'preclusive' imperialism – annexing territory to forestall a rival.

* Imperialism was also closely linked to prestige. Colonies came to be regarded as status symbols. Great power status, previously measured in terms of population, military capacity and industrial strength, now came to include overseas possessions – 'painting the map red'. Caprivi, Bismarck's successor, said many Germans believed that 'once we came into possession of colonies, then purchased an atlas and coloured the continent of Africa blue, we would become a great people'. The acquisition of Tunisia by France in 1880–81 was hailed as a sign that 'France is recovering her position as a great power'.

In the 1890s public opinion in Britain and elsewhere became an added force behind imperial expansion. 'Jingoism', an assertive form of nationalism, was encouraged (if not promoted) by the popular press. For example, the *Daily Mail* capitalised on 'the depth and volume of public interest in Imperial questions' of its one million readers. In France, where public opinion had been largely apathetic to imperialism before the 1890s, nationalism allegedly made many Frenchmen imperialists. Colonial societies and commercial pressure groups naturally took advantage of this mood to push governments into yet more colonial acquisitions.

The baleful influence of Social Darwinism was also felt on attitudes to colonies and native societies. The maxim 'survival of the fittest', when applied to the human rather than animal kingdom, acted as a justification for colonialism. Superior races – the Europeans – were obviously destined to rule over inferior ones. Britain was 'the greatest of governing races the world has ever seen', in Chamberlain's view. The obverse of this expansionist, self-confident feeling was the fear of decadence and decline. Jules Ferry made the point explicitly when he warned that unless France acquired colonies 'we shall take the road leading to decadence – we shall meet the fate of Spain'. The future, according to Chamberlain, lay with the great empires – 'and there is no greater empire than the British Empire', he added modestly. Clearly, nationalism was transforming itself into imperialism.

6 The Causes of the Scramble for Africa

The partition of Africa can be explained, in part, by some of the motives ascribed to imperialism in general. Nevertheless, some historians have searched for a more specific explanation of it. The 'classic' explanation is that offered by Robinson and Gallagher, who argued that British policy in Africa was essentially a defensive reaction to a series of local crises. The main consideration for the British government in these crises was, in their view, the security of the route to India. Their interpretation of the situation in southern Africa, in which they stressed the crucial importance of the Cape to imperial interests, has been generally accepted. On the other hand, their view that Egypt acted as a catalyst to the partition of tropical Africa has been widely criticised. Their notion of a 'chain reaction', in which French resentment at the British occupation of Egypt in 1882 activated a latent rivalry in West Africa, is not sound. French expansion from Senegal, which began in 1879, clearly pre-dated the crisis over Egypt.

* The view that it was rival claims to the Congo that sparked off the Scramble for Africa is more convincing. Firstly, the interests of at least four European states were involved, not just two as in the case of Egypt. Secondly, Bismarck's role in provoking the Scramble is given due prominence in this interpretation since Germany played an active part in the Congo dispute. Thirdly, the creation of a Franco-German front against Britain's attempt to exclude them from the Congo introduced great power diplomacy into the situation in Africa. An additional link between the Congo dispute and the partition of

Africa is the Berlin West Africa Conference of 1884–85, at which the ground rules for partition were laid down as well as a settlement of the Congo issue itself. Taken together, these four factors indicate that rival claims to the Congo played a more important part in initiating the Scramble than the Anglo-French dispute over Egypt.

A third line of enquiry has sought for an explanation of the timing of the Scramble. The key factor in the situation in the 1880s was, according to Sanderson, the decline of British 'paramountcy' in Africa. Until the late 1870s, Britain had succeeded in maintaining an informal influence over most of Africa south of the Sahara. In the 1880s this was challenged. Military defeats in Asia and Africa coinciding with a decline in relative naval power were interpreted as signs of British weakness. Bismarck concluded that there would not be much resistance to joint Franco-German pressure. He had reason to resent British pretensions to influence over most of Africa – the muddle over South West Africa and the attempt to exclude Germany and France from the Congo. British paramountcy collapsed like a house of cards when she agreed to an international conference. But its collapse left a void. In this unstable situation Africa was 'up for grabs'. Protectorates were being proclaimed over African territory and some mechanism was needed to settle rival claims. The solution was the Berlin Conference. This marked the formal beginning of the partition of Africa.

* The Scramble for Africa cannot be explained satisfactorily without some reference to changes taking place in Africa. Imperialism in general is no longer viewed exclusively in terms of economic or political pressures emanating from Europe. The traditional 'Eurocentric' approach is being modified by increasing recognition of the importance of changes at the 'periphery', as Fieldhouse calls it. Imperialism is therefore increasingly seen as, in part, a response to a series of local crises and changing situations within Africa itself. In the last twenty years African historians have contributed greatly to the awareness of these situations.

European governments were at times responding to crises that arose in different parts of Africa. In Egypt, the growth of an Egyptian nationalist movement forced Britain and France to decide between losing influence or intervention. Britain chose the latter, ostensibly to defend the Suez canal. In southern Africa a succession of crises seemed to put at risk strategic interests at the Cape. Most of these crises stemmed from the expansionist drives of European settlers. The French government faced similar problems from expansionists (especially the military) in Algeria and Senegal. In West Africa, problems arose when stable relationships between Europeans and Africans were upset by changes in the nature, or profitability, of existing patterns of trade. Two general conclusions may be drawn from current trends in the study of imperialism in Africa. Firstly, although economic imperialism is of relevance to European activity in Africa, it may be necessary to regard it as a quite separate factor from the European diplomacy of the Scramble. Secondly, the partition stemmed from an interaction between Europeans and Africans; it is not just a question of the impact of Europe on the Dark Continent.

7 The Effect of Colonial Rivalries on International Relations

Colonial rivalries inevitably had a great impact on relations between the great powers in this period. Indeed, apart from the Bulgarian crisis of 1885–87, the focal points of international tension were to be found in Africa and the Far East, rather than in Europe, for much of the period from about 1884 to 1904. During most of these years Britain's imperial rivalries with France and Russia were the key factor in international relations. Germany, however, failed to take advantage of Britain's difficulties to improve her own position in international affairs. Although Russia's defeat by Japan in 1905 tilted the balance of power in Europe in Germany's favour, this was offset by the marked improvement in Anglo-French and Anglo-Russian relations from about 1904 onwards.

Anglo-French relations underwent a dramatic change as a result of colonial rivalry. From 1870 until about 1884, Britain and France had no major quarrels and usually cooperated in international affairs. The next two decades, however, were marked by continual friction and tension, especially in Africa, bringing them to the verge of war. Hostility between Britain and Russia, on the other hand, was nothing new. In the context of Anglo-Russian relations it is important to remember that Russian activities and intrigues in regions bordering India in the 1870s and 1880s continued to cause Britain considerable alarm. In essence, the focus of conflict, apart from the continuing problem of the defence of India, was transferred from the Near East to the Far East. During this period of colonial rivalry the Franco-Russian Alliance of 1892–94 was more obviously anti-British in its operation than anti-German. By 1907, however, Britain had concluded agreements with both of her main colonial rivals.

 * 'Africa', complained Lord Salisbury, 'was created to be the plague of foreign offices'. If rivalry in West Africa impaired Anglo-French relations, the friction over Egypt strained them to near breaking point. The economic interests of Britain and France in West Africa were too small to justify war. Prestige was the crux of the matter. The danger was that a local incident could flare up into a crisis if public opinion, enflamed by the press, insisted that 'national honour' was at stake. Both sides engaged in rather reckless 'brinkmanship', raising the spectre of war on the Niger, until the agreement of 1898. By this date the crisis centre had shifted to the Nile.

Britain's refusal to revive the Anglo-French partnership (the Dual Control) after her military intervention in Egypt in 1882 was a severe blow to French pride. France could claim genuine cultural and sentimental ties with Egypt dating back to Napoleonic times. In the 1860s a Frenchman, de Lesseps, had built the Suez Canal. French self-esteem would only be satisfied by a British withdrawal from Egypt. Having failed to persuade the British, France attempted to exert pressure through the Fashoda expedition. By 1898, however, Britain was resolved to stay in Egypt. One reason for this was that Britain regarded signs of Franco-Russian co-operation in the Mediterranean in the 1890s as a serious threat to her strategic interests. In 1898, Britain would have gone to war with France rather than give way.

* The Fashoda crisis ended an era of illusions. Good relations between Britain and France had to be based on France's acceptance of Britain's position in Egypt. The important lesson which the French colonialists (but not the foreign minister) drew from Fashoda was that France should barter Egypt in exchange for French predominance in Morocco. This was the basis of the Anglo-French *entente*, or colonial agreement of 1904. Paradoxically, therefore, acute rivalry in Africa and Asia transformed international relations in the opposite way to what might be expected. By 1907 Britain and Russia had concluded an *entente*. By 1914, the Anglo-French colonial understanding had become almost an alliance, largely as a result of Germany's decision to make an issue out of France's ambitions in Morocco (see p. 99 and 108).

* The effect of colonial rivalries on Germany's relations with other powers was rather ambiguous. Germany seemed to use Africa partly as a means to an end – the furtherance of her diplomatic interests in Europe. In Africa Bismarck could find opportunities to conciliate France and to distract her from the grievance of Alsace-Lorraine. Hence his encouragement of France to take Tunisia in 1881. The thwarting of Italian ambitions there assured Franco-Italian hostility for a decade and induced Italy to join the Triple Alliance. Africa was also fertile ground for Franco-German co-operation against Britain. In the case of the Congo, Bismarck persuaded France to join Germany in 1884 in opposing Britain's rather dubious treaty with Portugal to exclude French and German interests. In similar fashion, the British stratagem of blocking access to the Upper Nile by the Anglo-Congolese Treaty of 1894 was frustrated by joint Franco-German protests.

Although there were no major disputes between Germany and Britain over Africa in Bismarck's time, he left a legacy of distrust of German policy. Making difficulties for Britain over Egypt was particularly resented as a sort of blackmail to secure concessions for Germany elsewhere. Germany was not regarded, however, as an undesirable colonial neighbour. The partitions of East Africa in 1886 and 1890 were negotiated in a fairly cordial spirit. German support for the Boers, on the other hand, was a source of serious tension, as the affair of the Kruger telegram in 1896 showed (see p. 89). As a means of improving Anglo-German relations, attempts were made in 1898 and again in 1912–13 to reach colonial agreements – at the expense of Portugal's colonies in Africa. The most serious clash in Africa was the clumsy attempt by Germany to provoke a crisis directed against French imperialism in Morocco in 1905 and in 1911 (see pp. 99 and 108). However, since Germany was not really seeking colonial gains in North Africa, these crises seem to belong to the realm of power politics rather than constituting genuine colonial rivalries.

There is thus no simple pattern to the diplomatic effects of Germany's colonial policy. In Bismarck's time, colonial issues were usually subordinate to his overall strategy. Colonial conflicts were thus kept within certain limits. After 1890, however, German overseas policy became much less predictable and less restrained which ultimately had a damaging effect on Anglo-German relations.

* Great power rivalries in the Far East also had important effects on international relations in the period 1895 to 1905. Russia was the only European power to become involved in war, but her rivalry with Britain resulted in tension over Port Arthur in 1897–98 and over Manchuria in 1900–01. The first crisis was initiated by Germany's seizure of Kiaochow in 1897–98, which Britain wrongly interpreted as a sign that Germany intended to play a major role in Far Eastern affairs. British hopes of an alliance with Germany to resist Russian expansion in China were therefore based on a misapprehension. The German government was happy to see Russia embroiled in the Far East – at a safe distance from the East Prussian frontier. Awakened to the realities of the situation in the Far East by Germany's assertion of total indifference to the fate of Manchuria in 1901, Britain turned to Japan. It might be suggested that the British ministers had been slow to see that an alliance with Japan was the obvious solution to their predicament. The Kaiser certainly thought so when he commented 'The noodles have had a lucid interval at last!'

There is less certainty whether the Anglo-Japanese Alliance of 1902 should be regarded as marking the end of Britain's 'Splendid Isolation'. In one sense it obviously did. Britain had now abandoned her traditional policy of avoiding 'entangling alliances' in peace time. The serious implications of the treaty with Japan were voiced by Lord Salisbury: 'It involves a pledge on our part to defend Japanese action in Korea. . . against France and Russia, no matter what the *casus belli* may be. There is no limit; and no escape. We are pledged to war.' On the other hand, this alliance was restricted in scope: it was a regional pact, limited to the Far East. Historians, including A J P Taylor, have therefore argued that the alliance did not impair Britain's freedom to maintain her isolation from her continental rivals. This is not quite accurate. In 1903 Britain, as the ally of Japan, feared she might become involved in war against France, as the ally of Russia. The commitment to Japan acted consequently as a catalyst to the negotiations for an entente with France. Salisbury's son disagreed with the view of these two alliances given in a speech in 1905 by Lansdowne, his father's successor at the foreign office, as this letter to Balfour indicates:

1 Lansdowne's speech on Tuesday was an important one. He . . .
    declared in effect that we had abandoned the policy of isolation,
    not only in Asia but also in Europe: that we must do as other
    Powers do, who are distributed in groups: that the Japanese
5 treaty and the French agreement have carried this change of
    policy into effect: and he almost treated these two instruments,
    though no doubt different in form, as substantially similar.
      All this is, of course, largely true, but I should be inclined to
    take some exception to the last. Circumstances no doubt have
10 driven us in respect to France further than we intended. There
    can be no doubt that originally French policy was wholly
    different from the Japanese. The latter, on the face of it, though
    defensive only, was essentially military. The former had its
    sanction and was intended to have its sanction in diplomatic
15 measures alone.
      In truth the French agreement was not a departure from our
    previous foreign policy, but strictly in accordance with it. For
    the last twenty years we have been engaged with different
    Powers, notably with Germany and with France, in adjusting
20 conflicting claims, and in bargaining so as to get rid of causes
    of friction and if I spoke about our agreement with France, I
    should treat it rather as a development of past policy than as a
    new departure.

Russia's defeat by Japan in 1905 had serious repercussions for international relations. Russia's prestige suffered a major blow and her military and naval capacity were greatly reduced. The outbreak of revolution in Russia in 1905, in protest against the incompetence of the Tsarist regime, weakened her further. Russia was therefore unable to play her full part as a great power in European affairs for several years after 1905. Germany took advantage of this in the crisis over Morocco and again in 1908–09 in the Bosnian affair. Furthermore, checked in the Far East, Russian ambitions turned back once more to the Near East. Balkan crises were back on the agenda of international affairs.

Imperial rivalries in Africa and Asia were not without their dangers but at least they were played out at a safe distance and did not usually involve questions of security and survival. In 1905 the centre of gravity

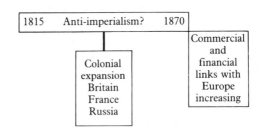

1815 Anti-imperialism? 1870

Colonial expansion Britain France Russia

Commercial and financial links with Europe increasing

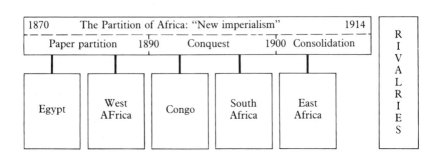

1870 The Partition of Africa: "New imperialism" 1914

Paper partition 1890 Conquest 1900 Consolidation

Egypt | West AFrica | Congo | South Africa | East Africa

R I V A L R I E S

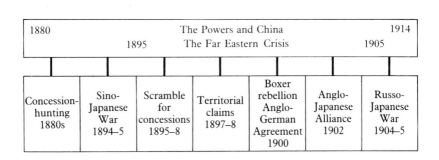

1880 The Powers and China 1914
1895 The Far Eastern Crisis 1905

Concession-hunting 1880s | Sino-Japanese War 1894–5 | Scramble for concessions 1895–8 | Territorial claims 1897–8 | Boxer rebellion Anglo-German Agreement 1900 | Anglo-Japanese Alliance 1902 | Russo-Japanese War 1904–5

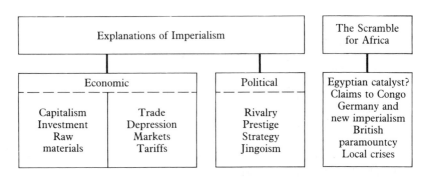

Explanations of Imperialism

The Scramble for Africa

Economic | Political

Capitalism Investment Raw materials | Trade Depression Markets Tariffs | Rivalry Prestige Strategy Jingoism

Egyptian catalyst? Claims to Congo Germany and new imperialism British paramountcy Local crises

Summary – Colonial Rivalries, 1870–1914

of international affairs returned to Europe when Germany, quite gratuitously, raised the spectre of war against France. This was *Weltpolitik* in action.

Making notes on 'Colonial Rivalries, 1870–1914'

Since the time-span of this chapter, 1870–1914, overlaps with that of the previous one (1871–90) as well as that of the next chapter (1890–1914), you will find some references to events or situations that you have already read about and others which you will encounter in more detail later. This applies particularly to aspects of great power rivalries and their effect on international relations. You may think it worthwhile to create a system of cross-references for this. Although the Partition of Africa (section 3) is an important part of the chapter, you could regard much of the text as an aid to understanding this complex topic rather than requiring detailed notes. The section on China complements the study of Africa and illustrates some key aspects of European imperialism. Close study of the maps is advisable.

When reading the chapter you should pay careful attention to the reasons for, and effects of, colonial rivalries and the causes of the 'Scramble' for Africa, as well as the use of the phrase, the 'new imperialism'. The following headings and sub-headings should provide a suitable framework for your notes:
1.   European states and colonies before 1870
1.1. Anti-imperialism in Britain
1.2. British colonial gains pre-1870
1.3. Reasons for expansion
2.   Africa 1815–70
2.1. Economic links with Europe pre-1870
3.   The partition of Africa
3.1. Egypt
3.2. Anglo-French rivalry in West Africa
3.3. The Congo
3.4. German intervention in Africa
3.5. Rivalries on the Nile and the Niger in 1890s
3.6. Britain, Germany and the Boers in South Africa
3.7. Rivalries 1900–14
4.   The powers and China
4.1. Economic interests – trade and investment
4.2. China avoids partition
4.3. The Anglo-Japanese Alliance, 1902
4.4. Conclusion
5.   Explanations of imperialism
5.1. Markets and raw materials
5.2. Economic imperialism

Answering essay questions on *'Colonial Rivalries, 1870–1914'*

Questions on this topic tend to focus on one of four issues: the causes of imperialism; the reasons for the partition of Africa; the nature of colonial activities; and the effects of colonial rivalries on international relations. Only very rarely is a question asked which combines two of these issues. The commonest questions are those that ask for an explanation of imperialism or of the Scramble for Africa. Study the following questions, which have been arranged on the basis of the four issues:

1 Why was the late nineteenth century an age of 'imperialism'?
2 Account for 'the new imperialism' of the European powers in the period 1870–1914.
3 Why did the nations of continental Europe expand overseas in the late nineteenth century?
4 'The flag followed the trade.' Discuss this explanation of the 'new imperialism'.
5 To what extent can the imperialist ambitions of the European powers between 1880 and 1914 be explained in economic terms?
6 What motives lay behind the 'Scramble for Africa' by the European powers?
7 What prompted the continental powers to participate in the 'Scramble for Africa'?
8 'The motives for the partition of Africa were diplomatic rather than economic.' Discuss this statement.
9 'Non-economic factors were of little importance in bringing about the 'Scramble for Africa'.' How valid is this statement?
10 Explain and illustrate the growing interest of the European powers in either a) Africa or b) China in the late nineteenth century.
11 In what ways did the 'Scramble for Africa' affect relations between the European powers during this period?
12 To what extent did colonial enterprise divert European nations from their other rivalries in the period 1870–1914?

You will probably have spotted that, in addition to dealing with the four issues mentioned earlier, each of these questions falls into one of the three categories, or 'types', which were discussed at the end of the previous chapter on Bismarck's foreign policy. Thus, of the five questions asked on the causes of imperialism, question 1 is a 'direct' question, question 4 is a 'challenging statement', while question 5 is a 'how far/to what extent' type of question. If you need to refresh your memory about these three types and how to respond to them, refer to page 45.

An appropriate response to question 1 would be to make a list of five or six main points, or paragraph headings, that you would use as a basis for an explanation of imperialism. Then group them under headings, such as 'economic' and 'political' motives, and arrange them in order of importance. What examples would you choose as 'evidence' for each point? How would you define 'imperialism'? Question 2 requires an explanation of the term 'new imperialism', but otherwise could be answered in the same way as question 1. Look now at question 3. Would the exclusion of Britain mean you would need to make changes in the list of points you drew up for the first question? For example, do you think that political factors played a more important role in the colonial expansion of continental states than in the case of Britain? Questions 4 and 5 require you to argue a case *for* and *against* economic factors being the motive behind imperialism. Using the points you listed for the first question, under the headings 'economic' and 'political', make an essay plan for an answer to question 5. Add an indication of the main point you would make in the introduction and conclusion.

Look again at the questions on the Scramble for Africa (6 to 9). What additions would you want to make to the list of paragraph points that you noted down for the questions about imperialism in general? Refer to your notes (under heading 6) for some possible additional factors. Are any points on your list not relevant to Africa? If you now re-arrange your list of paragraph points so they appear in order of importance, you should have the basis for an answer to question 6. Would any changes be necessary for an answer to question 7, because it excludes Britain? The next two questions (8 and 9) are both 'challenging statements', so your answer would have to be presented as an argument *for* and *against* the statement. Clearly, you can use the same line of argument for both questions – but would you change the way you presented it? Question 10 is one of the few questions that asks for illustrations of colonial activity, as well as an explanation of it. Some well-chosen examples would suffice, such as Bismarck's colonial policy, perhaps, for 10a. Would you explain European interest in China (10b) in the same terms as you would for Africa – or would you place more stress on economic factors such as investment?

Questions 11 and 12, which focus on the effects of colonial rivalries, do so in rather different ways. In answer to question 11, what main points, backed by evidence, would you make? Anglo-French rivalries ought to be near the top of your list, perhaps followed by the 'Egyptian lever'. In answer to question 12, you may be able to think of some examples that relate to the Bismarck era. The question will be considered more fully later (see p. 144), since it involves not only colonial rivalries, but also European affairs in the period 1890–1914.

Source-based questions on *'Colonial Rivalries, 1870–1914'*

1 The 'Egyptian Lever', 1886–87
Read carefully the extracts from Salisbury's letter and the ambassador's despatch given on pages 56 and 59. Answer the following questions:
a) These extracts illustrate the nature and working of the 'Egyptian Lever'. What was this?
b) What is meant in the second extract (line 6) by the departure 'from this traditional policy two years ago'?
c) What was Salisbury's opinion about Britain's involvement in Egypt? Why did he not argue for withdrawal?
d) How far are the generalisations contained in the first extract substantiated by the detailed evidence of the second extract?
e) How do the tones of the two extracts differ?

2 Great power rivalry in China, 1900
Read carefully the extracts from the Chamberlain Memorandum and the Anglo-German Agreement, given on pages 68–69. Answer the following questions:
a) What was Chamberlain's policy, as described in the first extract, for protecting British interests in China?
b) Were the terms of the Anglo-German Agreement in conformity with Chamberlain's policy? Explain your answer.
c) What were the implications of the fourth point in the Agreement?
d) On what basis could it be argued that the Agreement was hardly worth the paper it was written on?
e) What criticisms could be made of Chamberlain's policy, as described in his Memorandum?

3 Explanations of imperialism
Read carefully the extracts from the writings of Hobson and Lenin, given on pages 70–71, and examine the *Punch* cartoon reproduced on page 60. Answer the following questions:
a) In what ways are the explanations of imperialism given by Hobson

and Lenin i) similar to each other, and ii) different from each other?
b) What view of the nature of imperialism is suggested by the cartoonist through his portrayal of Africa and of the European powers? What is the significance of the snake in the foregound of the cartoon?
c) Would it be valid to describe the cartoonist, Hobson and Lenin as offering assertions rather than explanations? Justify your answer.
d) What economic explanations of imperialism have been given, other than those of Hobson and Lenin? What weaknesses do these explanations, as a group, have in common?
e) What do you consider to have been the most important single cause of imperialism in the late nineteenth century? Support your answer with evidence.

4 Britain and the end of isolation
Read carefully the extract from the letter to Balfour given on page 79 and study the *Punch* cartoon reproduced on page 98. Answer the following questions:
a) Who is Lansdowne? What is thought to be important about the speech he gave 'on Tuesday'?
b) What is meant by 'The former had its sanction . . . in diplomatic measures alone' (line 13)?
c) In what ways are Lansdowne and the cartoonist i) agreed, and ii) not agreed about the original nature of the Anglo-French *Entente*?
d) In what ways does the writer of the letter disagree with Lansdowne?
e) Which interpretation, Lansdowne's or the author of the letter's, is more convincing? Explain your answer.
f) What is the tone of the letter?

5 Anglo-French relations, 1898 and 1904
Study carefully the two *Punch* cartoons reproduced on pages 62 and 98. Answer the following questions:
a) Who is the monkey meant to represent? What is the artist's intention in characterising him in this way?
b) What is the attitude of the artist of the 'QUIT! – PRO QUO?' cartoon towards France, as revealed by, i) his choice of characters to represent Britain and France, and ii) the words spoken by the two characters?
c) In what ways are the attitudes towards France of the artists of the two cartoons, i) similar, and ii) different? Explain your answer in terms of the artists' characterisation of Britain and France, and of their placement of the characters in relation to one another.
d) Why was it possible for the British public to accept the change in perception of France between 1898 and 1904 from potential enemy to real friend?

CHAPTER 4

Weltpolitik and the Drift to War, 1890–1914

1 German Diplomacy after Bismarck, 1890–96

In the six years following Bismarck's fall, German foreign policy lacked a clear sense of direction and her international position was greatly weakened. France and Russia made an alliance but Germany failed to bind Britain more closely to the Triple Alliance. Indeed Anglo-German relations declined dramatically from their high water mark in 1890 to a nadir in 1896. The problem was not a shortage of ideas once Bismarck had gone; it was consistency that was most notably lacking. Above all, the German leaders seemed to lack the skill to translate ideas into successful policies.

 * The 'New Course', which Bismarck's successor as Chancellor, Caprivi, attempted to pursue from 1890 to 1894, was a deliberate rejection of Bismarck's system. In general, it was intended to simplify German policy by eliminating the 'criss-cross of commitments' contained within the Bismarckian system, while in particular, Caprivi's aim was to persuade Britain to join the Triple Alliance. The most crucial feature of this period was the decision taken in 1890 not to renew the Reinsurance Treaty of 1887 with Russia. This was mainly due to Holstein, a senior official in the foreign ministry who, partly because of Caprivi's lack of experience of foreign affairs, exercised great influence over German policy. He persuaded the Chancellor and the Kaiser that the treaty was incompatible with Germany's commitments to her other allies. Because of this, Holstein argued, Russia could blackmail Germany by the threat to reveal the terms of the treaty to them. This decision prepared the ground for the major event of the decade in international affairs – the Franco-Russian Alliance of 1892–94.

France, a democratic Republic, and Russia, ruled by an autocratic Tsar, seem rather strange bedfellows – an 'unholy alliance', perhaps? A common fear of Germany would be the obvious explanation for this unnatural union. In the early 1890s, however, Russia had no serious conflict of interest with Germany and wanted to renew the 1887 treaty with her. The initiative therefore came from France who, for the sake of security from a German attack, wanted a military agreement with Russia. The French proposals did not appeal to the Tsar's more conservative ministers. However, the blocking of a French loan to the Tsarist government, in dire financial straits in 1891, obliged Russia to respond more favourably to the idea of an alliance. To overcome the absence of an identity of interest, two separate agreements were made – a political *entente* in 1891, followed by a military convention a year later. The political agreement was anti-British in intent, aligning France with Russia in imperial disputes. In the military convention, France and Russia promised mutual support if either were attacked by Germany, and immediate mobilisation in response to mobilisation by one or more of the Triple Alliance powers. France had to wait until 1894 for the Tsar's confirmation of the alliance – a sign of his displeasure at the Panama Scandal – a financial scandal that broke out in 1892.

★ The Franco-Russian Alliance brought to an end the Bismarckian system by which Germany had directed the affairs of Europe for two decades. France had now broken out from the 'quarantine' imposed on her by Bismarck. This was manifested to the world when a Russian squadron visited Toulon, the French naval base in the Mediterranean, in October 1893. Although the visit had a more immediate impact on Britain, for whom the Mediterranean was a vital imperial waterway to India and the Far East, the ultimate significance of the Dual Alliance was not lost on Berlin. Germany now faced the prospect of a war on two fronts.

The potential danger to Germany from the Franco-Russian Alliance could have been partially offset by the conclusion of an Anglo-German Alliance. British naval power and German military strength would have made a formidable combination. Moreover, Germany could expect to enlist British support against Russia for the defence of Austro-Hungarian interests in the Balkans. Yet although an alliance with Britain was a major element of Caprivi's 'New Course', the German leaders failed to secure it.

The prospects for an alliance seemed good in the early 1890s when cordiality was the keynote of Anglo-German relations. In the Heligoland-Zanzibar Treaty of 1890, Germany made generous concessions to satisfy British claims in East Africa. The Kaiser, in one of his pro-British moods, declared 'Africa is not worth a quarrel between Britain and Germany'. The Germans, however, failed to capitalise on this mood, believing that sooner or later Britain would have to seek an alliance. One obstacle in particular in the early 1890s which they did not appreciate was the aversion of Lord Salisbury, the Conservative prime minister and foreign secretary (1887–92; 1895–1900), to a formal alliance. His attitude has been summed up as wanting 'the advantages of friendship without the encumbering engagements of an alliance'. Once again, Holstein's influence was evident in the assumption that the sheer logic of Britain's rivalry with France and Russia would compel her to seek the support of the Triple Alliance powers.

An opportunity for creating closer ties with Britain arose in 1894 when the then British prime minister, Lord Rosebery, reassured the Austrians of his determination to defend Constantinople. But to ensure that Britain had to deal with Russia only, he required a commitment from Germany that she would keep France in check. In Berlin, however, this was regarded as a clumsy British trick. Caprivi wrongly suspected that Britain wanted a free hand to attack Russia whenever she chose, leaving Germany to face the risk of war with France. According to A J P Taylor, July 1894 was a historic date, marking 'the end of Anglo-Austrian co-operation against Russia'. Since Bismarck had attached importance to securing British support for the defence of Austro-Hungarian interests in the Balkans, it is strange that the chance to strengthen the links between Britain and the Triple Alliance was missed in 1894.

The German leaders were too confident that circumstances would force Britain to join the Triple Alliance on their terms. They therefore believed that Britain needed Germany more than Germany needed Britain. This was a miscalculation. As Rosebery recognised in 1894, the solution to most of Britain's overseas problems was to strengthen the navy. Although British ministers favoured co-operation with Germany, they were not prepared to accept dictation from Berlin. Britain's friendship was readily obtainable, but the German leaders were not satisifed with this. It was a case of 'all or nothing'. Having failed to secure a formal alliance by a few concessions in the early 1890s, they resorted later to pressure and coercion. As a consequence, Anglo-German relations deteriorated in the course of the decade.

* After Caprivi's resignation in 1894, the German government, despairing of Britain as an ally, turned to alternative lines of policy. The first was an attempt to turn the clock back to 1890 by seeking a *rapprochement* with Russia. Despite the conclusion of a commercial treaty favourable to Russian agrarian interests, the attempt failed. The Tsar would not jettison the alliance with France for what might be a passing phase in German economic and foreign policy. Even so, Russo-German relations were quite cordial for some years, helped by the fact that the new Tsar, Nicholas II, got on well with the Kaiser. Having failed to secure an agreement with Russia, the Germans tried a different course. In some respects this was almost a preview of the 'world policy' pursued from 1897 to 1914. It amounted to a policy of meddling almost at random in colonial issues such as boundary disputes in the Sudan, the future of the Portuguese colonies in Africa, and quarrels over the Samoan Islands, accompanied by a bullying and offensive tone. Hence even when Germany had reasonable grounds for her actions, her style of diplomacy caused considerable offence as well as puzzlement at her motives. This was particularly the case in London. Salisbury is reported by the ambassador to Berlin to have said in 1895:

1 The conduct of the German Emperor is very mysterious and difficult to explain. There is a danger of his going completely

off his head . . . In commercial and colonial matters Germany
was most disagreeable. Her demand for the left bank of the
5 Volta (in the Gold Coast) was outrageous, so much so that he
thought it must have been the idea of the Emperor himself as
no responsible statesman could have put it forward. The rudeness
of German communications, much increased since Bismarck's
time, was perhaps due to the wish of smaller men to keep up
10 the traditions of the great Chancellor . . . In the Far East, the
Germans are up to every sort of intrigue, asking for concessions
and privileges of all sorts, with a view to cutting us out.

The culmination of this type of diplomacy was the affair of the
'Kruger Telegram' in 1896. The Jameson raid, an armed attack
(initiated by Cecil Rhodes, using British South Africa Company police)
to incite an uprising in Johannesburg against the Boers, was an illegal
act against the Transvaal state. As thousands of Germans were active
in the commercial life of the country, it was quite proper for the
German government to express concern over the fate of the Boer
Republic. Their manner of proceeding, however, was very clumsy.
Once Berlin was informed that the raid had not been approved by
the British government, the matter should have been allowed to rest.
Instead, the German foreign minister invited French and Russian co-
operation against Britain, hoping that this sort of pressure would
induce her to join the Triple Alliance. When the French and Russians
refused, the Kaiser took control of German policy. He decided to
send a telegram, to Kruger, the Boer President, supporting the
independence of the Transvaal, couched in these terms:

1 I would like to express my sincere congratulations that you and
your peoples have succeeded, without having to invoke the help
of friendly powers, in restoring peace with your own resources
in face of armed bands which have broken into your country as
5 disturbers of the peace and have been able to preserve the
independence of your country against attacks from outside.

This message caused great offence in Britain because the Transvaal
was not a fully independent state. In 1884 it had accepted British
control over its external relations. The British press consequently
treated the Kaiser's action as a gross interference in Britain's imperial
affairs. According to the German ambassador in London, 'If the
government had wished for war . . . it would have had the whole of
public opinion behind it'.

* In 1896 Anglo-German relations, so cordial in 1890, were at a
nadir. But it was not only Anglo-German relations that had deteriorated
in the six years since Bismarck's fall. In 1890 Berlin was the focal
point of European diplomacy through the Triple Alliance and the
Reinsurance Treaty. By 1896, however, France, no longer isolated,

was the ally of Russia, but Britain had not drawn closer to the Triple Alliance powers, so that Germany's international position was much less secure. It seems clear that since 1890 German diplomacy had been a conspicuous failure.

In the eyes of important sections of German opinion, however, this was not the case. Caprivi's quiet diplomacy had not been very popular, but the erratic, assertive course of German diplomacy since 1894 provoked great enthusiasm in Germany. Admiral Müller summed up the situation in 1896 as follows:

1 General von Caprivi believed that Germany had no chance at all of becoming a world power, and consequently his policy was designed only to maintain Germany's position on the European continent. He was therefore acting quite logically in working at
5 home for the strengthening of the army, limiting the navy to the role of defending the coastline . . . and seeking good relations with England as the natural ally against Russia, the country which threatened Germany's position in Europe.

  Caprivi's policy, now so widely ridiculed, would have been
10 brilliantly vindicated by history if the German people were not coming to accept an entirely different opinion of their ability and duty to expand than that expressed in our naval and colonial development so far.

  Now, the Caprivi policy has been officially abandoned, and
15 the new Reich Government will hesitantly put to the nation the question – in the form of the new Navy Bill – whether the other policy, *Weltpolitik*, really can be adopted. Let us hope that this question receives an enthusiastic 'Yes' for an answer, but also that then a change comes over our external relations in favour
20 of an understanding with England.

In short, the German people wanted to see Germany transformed from a continental to a world power. The era of *Weltpolitik* had begun.

2 *Weltpolitik* and the End of British Isolation, 1897–1904

In 1897, Germany embarked on a 'World Policy' (*Weltpolitik*) that was, by intent, a rejection of the restrained 'continental policy' of the Bismarck era. The emphasis was now on expansion, especially overseas expansion, and the creation of a big navy. British proposals for an alliance were rejected in favour of a 'Free Hand'. Apart from a few initiatives on the world stage, German foreign policy amounted to little more than hoping to profit from Britain's imperial problems. *Weltpolitik* was not a success for Germany; by 1904 she had little to show for the new policy. Britain, on the other hand, having clashed with France over the Nile in 1898, with Russia in the Far East and with the Boers in South Africa from 1899–1902, had made an alliance with Japan in 1902 and settled her colonial rivalries with France in 1904.

* *Weltpolitik* did not have a very precise meaning, but it is a convenient term to sum up the expansionist phase of German policy that began in the late 1890s. 1897 is usually regarded as marking its beginning. In that year, the Kaiser asserted his right to 'Personal Rule' and made two important changes in his ministers. Bülow was appointed to the foreign ministry and Admiral von Tirpitz to head the navy office. The latter appointment signified that Germany was to begin the construction of a powerful battle fleet. The role of the new foreign minister was twofold. Firstly, he was to foster good relations with Britain while the German fleet was in its infancy. Secondly, his more obvious task was to project Germany on to the world stage to satisfy the German people's craving for 'a place in the sun' – a tropical empire. The Kaiser, himself an enthusiast for expansion, said in 1898, 'Germany has great tasks to accomplish outside the narrow boundaries of old Europe'.

* What these 'great tasks' were is not very obvious. As Germany's army commander remarked at about this time: 'We are supposed to pursue *Weltpolitik*. If only we knew what it was supposed to mean.' Whether its content or ultimate objectives were ever clearly defined is still a matter of debate. Basically, there are two schools of thought on this issue. Historians who agree with Fritz Fischer (the initiator of the revived debate on German war guilt) see a sort of masterplan to *Weltpolitik*. They detect three main elements in it; one was the navy; the second was the plan for a Central African empire (*Mittelafrika*); and the third was the European economic zone scheme.

* The new German navy would demonstrate Germany's status as a World Power, thereby rallying popular support behind the Kaiser and government. The grandiose *Mittelafrika* scheme would enlarge Germany's colonial empire. Since most of Africa had already been partitioned by the late 1890s, this implied acquiring territory by negotiation or purchase. The most coveted areas to add to Germany's existing colonial territories were the Congo and the Portuguese colonies of Angola and Mozambique. The idea of a Central European economic zone, or customs union (*Mitteleuropa*), under German domination, was a quite different concept. Rarely defined with precision, it was usually conceived as including Austria-Hungary, the Balkan states, Turkey and the Near East. Related to this *Mitteleuropa* scheme was the plan to link the whole area together by a railway from Berlin to Baghdad.

* Fischer's critics point to the fact that *Weltpolitik* seems to have consisted of three unrelated projects, which suggests a lack of coherence in German policy rather than the existence of a master plan. The

apparent link between the navy and colonies was an illusion since the new fleet was designed for action in the North Sea.

Contemporary observers, as well as modern historians, were uncertain how to interpret *Weltpolitik*. Eyre Crowe, a Foreign Office official, commented on it in 1907 in these terms:

1 Either Germany is definitely aiming at a general political
    hegemony and maritime ascendancy, threatening the indepen-
    dence of her neighbours and ultimately the existence of England;
    Or Germany, free from any such clear-cut ambition and thinking
5 for the present merely of using her legitimate position and
    influence as one of the leading powers . . . is seeking to promote
    her foreign commerce . . . and create fresh German interests all
    over the world wherever and whenever a peaceful opportunity
10 offers, leaving it to an uncertain future to decide whether the
    occurrence of great changes in the world may not some day
    assign to Germany a larger share of direct political action over
    regions not now part of her dominions without that violation of
    the established rights of other countries which would be involved
15 in any such action under existing political conditions.

Behind the pursuit of *Weltpolitik* there lay, beyond doubt, a vague longing to be a World Power. But, the meanings the German people attached to the concept of world power were ill-defined and often inconsistent. The most obvious pressure for an expansionist policy came from the widespread consciousness in Germany of the nation's growing power. Second only to Britain as the world's largest trading and commercial nation, Germany also ranked second (after the USA) in the world as a great industrial nation. But this economic strength was not reflected in the size of her overseas empire. The German sense of grievance over this disparity was expressed by Admiral Müller in 1896 in these terms:

1 World history is now dominated by the economic struggle. This
    struggle has raged over the whole globe but most strongly in
    Europe, where its nature is governed by the fact that central
    Europe (*Mitteleuropa*) is getting too small and that the free
5 expansion of the peoples who live here is restricted as a result
    of the present distribution of the inhabitable parts of the earth
    and above all as a result of the world domination of England.
    The war which could – and many say must – result from this
    situation of conflict would . . . have the aim of breaking
10 England's world domination in order to lay free the necessary
    colonial possessions for the central European states who need to
    expand. . .

Furthermore, despite her economic strength, Germany's standing alongside the existing 'world empires' of the United States, the Russian

Empire and the British Empire was felt to be inadequate. Eyre Crowe
explained this attitude thus:

1   The colonies and foreign possessions of England . . . were seen
    to give to that country a recognised and enviable status in a
    world where the name of Germany . . . excited no particular
    interest . . . Such a state of things was not welcome to German
5   patriotic pride. Germany had won her place as one of the leading,
    if not in fact, the foremost power on the European continent.
    But over and beyond the European great powers there seemed
    to stand the 'world powers'. It was at once clear that Germany
    must become a 'world power'. . . .
10 Meanwhile, the dream of a colonial empire had taken deep
    hold on the German imagination. Emperor, statesmen, journalists,
    . . . economists . . . and the whole mass of . . . public opinion
    continue with one voice to declare: We must have real colonies
    . . . and we must have a fleet and coaling stations to keep
15 together the colonies we are bound to acquire.

It was pressures such as these which induced Bülow to assert: 'We
can't do anything other than carry out *Weltpolitik*'.

  * Many historians, however, especially Wehler and other German
scholars of the Fischer school, such as Berghahn and Geiss, have not
been satisfied with this simple explanation. They see Germany's
unstable and anachronistic socio-political system as the root cause of
Weltpolitik. 'German foreign policy after 1897', according to such a
view, 'must be understood as a response to the internal threat of
socialism and democracy'. They argue that to escape the political
consequences of industrialisation (i.e. democratisation of the regime)
the traditional ruling classes resorted to 'diversionary tactics'. These
were to distract opinion from domestic tensions and problems by
pursuing a prestige policy on a world scale. There is certainly no
shortage of contemporary comments which can be quoted in support
of this view. For example, Bülow said: 'Only a successful foreign
policy can help to reconcile, rally and unite.' Holstein, his adviser,
observed: 'The Kaiser's government needs some tangible success
abroad which will have a beneficial effect at home.' Tirpitz's navy
plan was supposedly intended, in part, 'as a political weapon against
the Social Democrats' – by rallying the people behind the fleet and
the Kaiser. In short, fear of the working class was the driving force
behind *Weltpolitik*. Imperialism was, according to this view, a substitute
for unwanted social change – hence the phrase 'social imperialism'.

  An alternative to this consensus view has recently been offered by
an American historian, David Kaiser. He claims that historians have
misunderstood both the domestic aims and foreign policy goals of
Weltpolitik. In a memorable phrase he suggests that *Weltpolitik* was 'a
patriotic umbrella, not a magic wand'. It was not intended to perform

a 'vanishing trick' on the Socialists, about whom Bülow was not very alarmed in this period, but to create a working compromise amongst those groups who were making the government's task in the *Reichstag* very difficult. The pursuit of prestige abroad was intended to rally the 'patriotic forces' – Conservatives, National Liberals and the Catholic Party – behind the government instead of pursuing their own selfish (and divisive) interests. Bülow's basic aim was to impress both public opinion and the Kaiser by a few cheap successes, in which appearances counted for more than realities. Hence a worthless acquisition, such as the Caroline Islands, could be presented as a triumph of German diplomacy, stimulating the people 'to follow Your Majesty along the path to world power and greatness', as Bülow put it. According to this view, German foreign policy from 1897 to 1904 was largely a 'public relations' exercise.

* This interpretation of the motives behind *Weltpolitik* may seem rather extreme in the way it scales down the grandiose aims attributed to German policy by other historians. It does, however, have the merit of making sense of some aspects of *Weltpolitik* that are otherwise rather puzzling. For example, if there was a master plan to *Weltpolitik*, why did the German government not pursue its objectives in a more consistent and coherent way? If, in fact, *Weltpolitik* had no very specific foreign policy goals, the inconsistencies in German policy are easier to understand – at least for us, if not for contemporaries.

Contemporary observers tended to attribute the vagaries of German diplomacy to the personality of the Kaiser. In this they were partly correct. Wilhelm II was a complex character whose moods were liable to change very rapidly and violently. As Bismarck commented: 'The Kaiser is like a balloon. If you do not hold fast to the string, you never know where he will be off to.' His changeability was very evident in his 'love-hate' relationship with Britain. For example, during the Boer War 1899–1902, the Kaiser proposed a 'continental league' directed against her but also offered advice to the British government on how to defeat the Boers. Furthermore, he insisted on making a death-bed visit to his grandmother, Queen Victoria, despite the rampant anglophobia in Germany. The visit made him a popular hero (temporarily at least) in Britain.

* It is important to remember that Wilhelm II 'possessed powers and prerogatives which were closer to those of George III than those of his uncle Edward VII'. If he had exercised these powers to act as the co-ordinator of Germany policy-making, he could have played a valuable role. Instead, he represented yet another voice alongside that of the Chancellor, foreign minister, foreign ministry officials such as Holstein, and army and navy chiefs. Consequently, the aims of German diplomacy were never fully defined, the priorities never clearly established. Two examples may suffice. Should Germany pursue an expansionist policy overseas by co-operation with Britain, or by

confrontation? Secondly, was it better to side with Britain or with Russia in world affairs? No firm decision was ever made on the basic options facing Germany at this time.

Clearly, the Kaiser was not the only one to blame for the lack of clear aims in German diplomacy in this era. If the foreign ministers of other states were puzzled by German policy, this was the price Bülow paid for his policy of the 'Free Hand'. This policy amounted to keeping Germany free of commitments to other states (other than her alliance partners) while waiting for something to turn up – preferably disasters – from which Germany could hope to profit. *Weltpolitik* was a strange mixture of reasonable aspirations and some justified claims, combined with ill-defined objectives.

This may help to explain why the achievements of German diplomacy in the period 1897 to 1904 were rather limited. Kiaochow was obtained from China as a naval base in 1897 and the Shantung province claimed as Germany's 'sphere of interest' for economic exploitation. She purchased a group of islands in the Pacific (the Carolines, Marshalls and Marianas) from Spain in 1898. Negotiations with Britain over the future of Portugal's empire in Africa seemed to offer the prospect of more substantial colonial gains which might have made a reality of the *Mittelafrika* idea. The British government, however, played a double game by averting the bankruptcy of Portugal on which German hopes were based. An acrimonious dispute with Britain over German claims to the Samoan Islands ended in 'simply a prestige victory', as a German colonial expert admitted in 1899. Although Germany won her claim to control the main island in the group, the commercial value of it was slight. Bülow admitted that 'the entire Samoan question has . . . no material but . . . a patriotic interest for us' – a good example, perhaps, of a 'public relations exercise'? A joint Anglo-German blockade of Venezuela in 1902–03 was a sign of the willingness of the two governments to co-operate but public opinion now began to cause complications. It was agreed that firm pressure was needed on the Venezuelan government which had defaulted on its foreign debts. But the bombardment of a port by the German flotilla created a storm in the British press, forcing the government to abandon the blockade.

The press, especially the Conservative newspapers, also frustrated the attempt by the Conservative government in England to co-operate with Germany in the Berlin-Baghdad railway scheme. The British government was willing to support this ambitious project which was designed to open up the Near East to European (especially German) economic penetration, on condition that certain key sections of the line were under international control. It was the pressure of 'this anti-German fever', as Lansdowne, Salisbury's successor as foreign secretary called it, that obliged the government to withdraw its support in 1903. If the British government was, at times, less than generous in its attitude towards German aspirations for more colonies this was partly because of the brusque methods employed. It was also a sign of concern at how public opinion might react to concessions made to Germany.

Clearly, public opinion in Britain and Germany was becoming a significant factor in Anglo-German relations during the years 1897 to 1904. Economic rivalry between the two great manufacturing and trading nations was keenly felt, aggravated by disputes over tariff policies. In Germany, anglophobia reached its height during the Boer War, 1899–1902. In Britain, anti-German feeling became quite pronounced in the early 1900s. This was partly a result of the second Navy Law of 1900, which doubled the size of the projected German fleet, giving rise to fears for Britain's naval supremacy.

* The growing antagonism had more serious implications for Germany than for Britain. An important element in German policy was to allay British suspicions while the German navy was being expanded. The Kaiser had done his best by successful visits to England. Bülow, on the other hand, had failed to 'square the circle' of combining an assertive, expansionist overseas policy with Anglo-German cordiality. At the root of this was Bülow's determination (unknown to the Kaiser) not to be drawn into an alliance with Britain, despite British desires for closer ties with Germany. Bülow was quite convinced that Britain's imperial rivalries with Russia and, to a lesser extent, with France must inevitably lead to war. It therefore followed that it would be a mistake for Germany to align herself with Britain and thereby antagonise Russia. All Germany had to do was to wait for the inevitable conflict from which she could then extract a high price for her favours. Hence Bülow's delight at the Fashoda crisis of 1898 between Britain and France and later at the outbreak of the Russo-Japanese war in early 1904. Britain, he assumed, would become involved as the ally of Japan. Although this 'wait and see' policy had a certain logic to it, it also contained a fatal flaw. It made no allowance for Britain resolving her imperial rivalries without war.

By the turn of the century leading Conservative ministers, especially Chamberlain, the very influential colonial secretary, shared Bülow's pessimistic appraisal of Britain's situation in the world. 'Splendid Isolation' seemed outmoded for 'the weary Titan', staggering under the too vast orb of his fate', as Chamberlain put it. His solution, pursued from 1898 to 1901, was an alliance with Germany, oblivious of the fact that Germany was unwilling to 'pull English chestnuts out of the Russian fire'. This was understandable since it made no sense for Germany to antagonise Russia in the Far East where, for the most part, her activities did not threaten the interests of Germany or her allies. Disappointed with Germany, British ministers slowly came to appreciate more fully the value of Japan as an ally to check Russian ambitions in China.

The Anglo-Japanese Alliance of 1902 seemed to mark the formal abandonment of Britain's 'isolation'. It also acted as a catalyst to the negotiations for an Anglo-French *entente*, or agreement. The British government became increasingly anxious, in the course of 1903, to reach an agreement with France as tension mounted between Russia and Japan. Lansdowne, the foreign secretary, was alarmed at the prospect that Britain and France might become involved in this conflict (as allies of the main protagonists) if they did not reach an accord. Once the French foreign minister had accepted that Egypt would have to be included in the bargaining, a basis for a colonial understanding existed. In return for a French undertaking not to obstruct British rule in Egypt, Britain accepted France's claim to a predominant influence in Morocco. The *Entente Cordiale* of 1904, whilst not constituting an alliance, indicated a mutual desire to terminate the friction that had persisted since the 1880s and a willingness to co-operate in the future. In anticipation of difficulties with Germany over Egypt, rather than Morocco, the agreement included a promise of mutual diplomatic support. By 1904, therefore, Britain's international position was much less precarious than it had been in 1897–98. She now had Japan as an ally and France as an *entente* partner, who might also be able to smooth Britain's path towards an agreement with Russia.

Although not anti-German in intent, the *Entente* had serious implications for Germany. No longer could Berlin count on the antagonism between Britain and France which had made them dependent on German goodwill. Holstein's comment that 'no overseas policy is possible against England and France' indicates that *Weltpolitik* had suffered a major setback from the Anglo-French accord. Even the 'silver lining' of the Russo-Japanese war turned out to be a false hope. German expectations rose as Russia turned to Berlin for support, but Bülow's hopes of a Russo-German alliance, were dashed by the Tsar's insistence on consulting France before concluding the alliance.

By the end of 1904, therefore, few of the aims of German diplomacy in 1897 had been achieved. Despite the fanfares, *Weltpolitik* had added little to Germany's overseas empire. On the other hand, the navy programme, a central element in the quest for world power status, was proving very popular in Germany. The flaw in Tirpitz's naval strategy was that the British Admiralty had realised by 1904, if not sooner, that 'the German fleet was designed for a possible conflict with Britain'. To meet the challenge, countermeasures were taken. As Prince Henry of Prussia noted in 1903, 'the cat is out of the bag'. By this time anti-German feeling was growing stronger in Britain. The chance for an Anglo-German alliance, which could have strengthened Germany's international position, had passed by 1902. One consolation for Germany was that Russia's involvement in the Far East and her *détente* with Austria in the Balkans had made Germany feel more

A MUTUAL SACRIFICE:

OR, L'AUTEL DU LIBRE ÉCHANGE.

secure in Europe. If the war against Japan weakened Russia's ability to play a major role in European affairs, Germany would be presented with an opportunity to alter the European balance of power in her favour. This would make up for some of the disappointments of the period 1897 to 1904.

3 Crises and Tension, 1905–9

A new and significant factor in the international situation between 1905 and 1909 was the temporary eclipse of Russia as a great power. This major upset in the balance of power was the result of Russia's defeat by Japan in the Far East and the outbreak of revolution at home. Russia's weakness gave Germany an opportunity to free herself from the sense of 'encirclement' which the Franco-Russian Alliance and the Anglo-French *Entente* had seemingly created around her. She attempted to break the *entente* by threatening France over Morocco in 1905. She also tried to weaken the Franco-Russian Alliance by seeking a defensive alliance with Russia. Having failed in both attempts, Germany exploited Russia's continuing weakness by forcing her to climb down in the Bosnian affair in 1909.

In the spring of 1905, Germany provoked a crisis ostensibly over Morocco but it was more fully an exercise in European power politics. The prime object was to inflict a diplomatic defeat on France, whose aspirations to make Morocco a French sphere of influence suffered a severe setback. In January 1905, a French mission had arrived in Fez, capital of Morocco, to induce the Sultan to accept a programme of reforms under exclusive French supervision. The French mission had aroused German fears that Morocco would become 'another Tunisia' – another French protectorate. If this happened, German commercial interests would suffer. As a dramatic way of asserting Germany's right to be consulted in such matters, the Kaiser landed at the Moroccan port of Tangier in March 1905. In declaring his intention of upholding the independence of Morocco, the German Emperor was throwing down a challenge to France's ambitions there.

This was made clear in mid-April when the German government demanded an international conference to review the question of Morocco. Germany based this demand on an international agreement signed in 1880, guaranteeing full commercial freedom in Morocco, so she had quite a good case. She also had a grievance that the French foreign minister had made no attempt to negotiate with Germany, as he had with other powers, about Morocco. Holstein, who played a key role in the crisis, made the point that 'If we allow our feet to be stepped on in Morocco without a protest, we simply encourage others to do the same somewhere else'. However, if Germany only wanted 'compensation' for French gains in Morocco, she could have used

normal diplomatic channels. It was her brusque, unorthodox methods
that caused unease.

★ The French and British governments were puzzled by Germany's
behaviour. They could not see the objectives of German policy. This
is not surprising, as the evidence suggests that the Germans provoked
the crisis without a clear idea of what they wanted to gain from it.
In Taylor's view, 'They wished to show that Germany could not be
ignored in any question in the world . . . But essentially they
speculated on some undefined success'. To understand the Moroccan
crisis it may be helpful to regard German policy as operating on two
levels. On the surface, they were demanding 'fair shares for all' in
Morocco and the right to be consulted about Morocco's fate. Their
hidden aim was to weaken, if not destroy, the Anglo-French *entente*.
This was to be achieved by demonstrating that Britain was not a
reliable or worthwhile ally. As Holstein put it, 'The French will only
consider approaching us when they see that English friendship is not
enough to obtain Germany's consent to the French seizure of Morocco'.

★ That Germany regarded the *entente* as a serious blow to her
overseas and continental interests is beyond dispute. When informed
of the substance of the *entente* in 1904 the German government had
officially disclaimed any territorial or political ambitions in Morocco,
providing her economic interests were respected. The German foreign
office, however, had described the *entente* as 'One of the worst defeats
for Germany policy since the Dual Alliance' of 1894. If the prime
object of German policy was to break the *entente*, there was a basic
logic to their actions. France, it was assumed, would be outvoted at
the international conference since other nations would not favour
French predominance in Morocco. So, humiliated by this check to
their aspirations, the French would recognise that co-operation with
Germany, not Britain, was essential. To accomplish this, it was
necessary to keep up the tension until the French government gave
in to Germany's demands. This aggressive policy was pursued through
the summer of 1905, backed by the unspoken threat of war. Some
historians believe, in fact, that the German Chief of Staff was hoping
the crisis would provide an excuse for an attack on France. The
evidence though is far from conclusive. But it is obvious that Russia's
weakness created a very favourable opportunity for a preventive war
against France.

Germany's actions, coupled with her refusal to negotiate directly
with France, created a panic in government circles in Paris. The
French army, disorganised by domestic political wrangles, was in no
condition to meet a surprise attack; nor could aid be expected from
her ally, Russia. So it was decided to sacrifice Delcassé – the architect
of the *Entente Cordiale* – to placate the Germans. His downfall is
regarded by some historians as an important motive in Germany's
policy in the crisis. The Kaiser attributed many of the recent setbacks

to German diplomacy to Delcassé's skilful mediation between Russia and England. His enforced resignation in June, however, served no purpose, except to cause dismay in London and jubilation in Berlin. Bülow was made a Prince! The German government still would not show its hand. Another month of tension and fruitless negotiation ensued. Finally, in July, the French prime minister gave way to the German demand for a conference that would meet in 1906 at Algeçiras. The 'security and independence' of Morocco would be decided by international agreement, not by Britain and France. Germany had demonstrated that she was a 'World Power' whose views could not be ignored. She had succeeded in inflicting a diplomatic defeat on France and the *entente*. All that remained· to be done was to ensure France's defeat at the conference.

Germany's motives puzzled, rather than alarmed, the British foreign secretary. On 9 April Lansdowne commented to the British ambassador in Berlin:

1   I entirely agree with you in looking upon the Emperor's Tangier
     escapade as an extraordinarily clumsy bit of diplomacy. . . .
     There can be no doubt that the Emperor was much annoyed by
     the Anglo-French Agreement . . . My impression is that the
5   German Government have really no cause for complaint against
     us or the French in regard to the Morocco part of the Agreement.
     We made no secret of its existence. It dealt exclusively with
     French and British interests in Morocco, and it provided adequate
     security for the interests of other Powers by maintaining the
10   policy of the 'open door' and equality of treatment, and the
     integrity of Morocco itself. What else does the Emperor want –
     unless perhaps it be to place orders for German guns?

Lansdowne was slow to grasp that the crisis might be a serious test for the *entente*. Diplomatic support was given to France in May and June 1905, as stipulated in the 1904 treaty. The Germans were warned that public opinion might react strongly if France seemed threatened. It was the rumour of German demands for a port in Morocco, however, that provoked the clearest signs of the British government's concern. On 25 May, Lansdowne reminded the French ambassador of the British government's attitude:

1   I observed that the moral . . . seemed to be that the French and
     British Governments should continue to treat one another with
     the most absolute confidence . . . and so far as possible discuss
     any contingencies by which we might in the course of events
5   find ourselves confronted and I cited as showing our readiness
     to enter into such timely discussion the communication recently
     made to the French Government . . . at a moment when the
     idea prevailed that Germany might be about to put pressure on

France in order to obtain the cession of a Moorish port.
10 I do not know that this account differs from that which you
have given to M. Delcassé, but I am sure that I succeeded in
making quite clear to you our desire that there should be full
and confidential discussion between the two Governments, not
so much in consequence of some acts of unprovoked aggression
15 on the part of another Power, as in anticipation of any
complications to be apprehended during the somewhat anxious
period through which we are at present passing.

Delcassé's resignation, regarded as a sign of French weakness,
dismayed the British. The *entente* seemed to be weakening under
German pressure. Moreover, its value to Britain as a restraining
influence on Russia was declining. Thanks to Japan's victories over
Russia in the Far East in the summer of 1905, British interests in
Asia were now more secure. There was not much contact between
the British and French governments in the autumn of 1905.

Although the Germans had won their point over Morocco, they
failed to capitalise on it. By September Germany's attitude to France
had noticeably softened. This change arose, in part, from the Kaiser's
attempt to pull off a personal diplomatic coup. For it to succeed, he
required France's goodwill, not her humiliation.   ⬅

* Russia's weakness gave the Kaiser just the opportunity he had
been waiting for to create closer ties between Germany and Russia.
Meeting the Tsar on the island of Björkö, in the Baltic, in late July,
he persuaded Nicholas II to sign a defensive alliance. There remained,
however, the awkward problem of how France, as Russia's ally, could
be fitted in to this new alignment. The Kaiser's solution was to suggest
that France be included in a sort of 'continental league' – directed
against Britain. For about two months it looked as though the Kaiser
had pulled off a great triumph. In October, however, the Tsar
suggested a delay in signing the treaty 'until we know how France
will look upon it'. French objections, which could not be ignored
given Russia's dependence on French loans, killed the project stone-
dead by November 1905.

The question of Morocco had still to be decided. German policy at
the beginning of the crisis, in April, was based on the assumption
that a majority of the powers would not wish to hand Morocco on a
plate to France. If the conference agenda was cleverly organised,
France's defeat could be assured in advance. By September, however,
the Kaiser and Bülow wanted to conciliate France – to secure her
participation in the Russo-German treaty agreed at Björkö. Bülow
therefore rejected Holstein's rigid stance on the conference programme,
saying, 'All that matters is to get out of this muddle over Morocco'
with as much prestige as possible. A further blow to Germany's
Morocco policy was still to come. By the time the conference met in

January 1906, a change of government in England had brought Sir
Edward Grey to the foreign office. The new Liberal foreign secretary
insisted on complete support for France at the Algeçiras conference
(even when she rejected reasonable compromises). His view of the
situation is shown in this report of a conversation with the French
ambassador on 31 January 1906:

1   The French Ambassador asked me again today whether France
    would be able to count upon the assistance of England in the
    event of an attack upon her by Germany.
        I said that I had spoken to the Prime Minister . . . and that
5   I had three observations to submit.
        In the first place, . . . our military and naval authorities had
    been in communication with the French, . . . so that, if a crisis
    arose, no time would have been lost for want of a formal
    engagement.
10 In the second place, . . . I had taken an opportunity of
    expressing to Count Metternich (the German ambassador) my
    personal opinion, which I understood Lord Lansdowne had also
    expressed to him as a personal opinion, that, in the event of an
    attack upon France by Germany, arising out of our Morocco
15 Agreement, public feeling in England would be so strong that
    no British Government could remain neutral. I urged upon M.
    Cambon (the French ambassador) that this . . . had produced
    in Berlin the moral effect which M. Cambon had urged upon
    me as being one of the great securities of peace and the main
20 reason for a formal engagement between England and France
    with regard to armed co-operation.
        In the third place, I pointed out to M. Cambon that at present
    French policy in Morocco . . . was absolutely free . . . that we
    left France a free hand and gave unreservedly our diplomatic
25 support on which she could count; but that, should our promise
    extend beyond diplomatic support, . . . I was sure my colleagues
    would say that we must . . . be free to press upon the French
    Government concessions or alterations of their policy which
    might seem to us desirable to avoid war. . . .
30 He eventually repeated his request for some form of assurance
    which might be given in conversation. I said that an assurance
    of that kind could be nothing short of a solemn undertaking.
    . . . I said that it might be that the pressure of circumstances –
    the activity of Germany, for instance – might eventually transform
35 the 'entente' into a defensive alliance . . . but I did not think
    that the pressure of circumstances was so great as to demonstrate
    the necessity of such a change yet.
        M. Cambon said the question was very grave and serious,
    because the German Emperor had given the French Government

40 to understand that they could not rely upon England, and it was very important to them to feel that they could.

After weeks of deadlock the Germans gave way when only Austria and Morocco supported them on a crucial vote. France secured virtual control of the police and the state bank. Germany had to be content with guarantees of commercial freedom, obtainable without a conference. Although France now had to act with some restraint in Morocco, Algeçiras was a bad blow for German prestige. As a demonstration of *Weltpolitik*, the Moroccan affair was a disaster. Although France was very vulnerable to pressure in the spring of 1905, Germany had extracted very little advantage from the situation. This was due to a mixture of miscalculation and inconsistency of aims. Direct negotiations with France could have produced positive gains, including 'compensation', if not in Morocco then in the French Congo. The First Moroccan Crisis, therefore, is a good example of the weaknesses of *Weltpolitik* – heavy-handed methods combined with uncertainty of aims.

 * The outcome was the opposite of what was intended. Far from weakening the Anglo-French *entente*, the crisis strengthened it. 'Cordial co-operation with France' became a basic principle of British foreign policy under Grey. Furthermore, he authorised 'military conversations' in January 1906 to consider how Britain might aid France if she were attacked by Germany. This has been called a 'revolution in European affairs'. For the first time in 40 years a British government considered despatching an expeditionary force to the Continent. Most historians agree with A J P Taylor that it was a true crisis. Most would also concur that Germany was not seeking an excuse for war against France in 1905. The threat of war, on the other hand, was freely used. 'The long Bismarckian peace' was over. Several states had contemplated war; an anticipation of things to come – albeit only a 'hint and a shadow'.

As a direct result of this crisis, Grey regarded Germany as a threat to the balance of power in Europe. This was a new anxiety that had not troubled British governments for several decades. The answer to this threat, Grey concluded was an *entente* including England, France and Russia so that, 'If it is necessary to check Germany it could then be done'.

Negotiations for an agreement with Russia began in April 1906, covering three disputed regions: Persia, Tibet and Afghanistan. Following her defeat in the Far East, Russia was more willing to compromise than in the past. Whereas British ministers had been trying to make an agreement with Russia since at least 1897, many of the Tsar's advisers had not seen much advantage to Russia in reducing tension with Britain. The new Russian foreign minister, Izvolsky, however, conscious of Russia's weakness, was anxious to improve her relations with Britain and the other powers.

After lengthy negotiations from April 1906 to August 1907, agreement was reached on the main issues. Persia was divided into three zones: a Russian zone adjacent to her frontier; a British zone in the south-east covering the Indian border; and a neutral zone separating the two. The agreements on Tibet and Afghanistan also contributed to the security of India, long the key issue in Anglo-Russian antagonism. In effect, both sides agreed not to meddle, to the disadvantage of the other, in the internal affairs of these two 'buffer states'. The Anglo-Russian convention of August 1907 should have begun a new era in Britain's relations with Russia, but Russia cheated persistently on the Persian agreement.

Despite this, Grey strove hard to minimise the damage to Anglo-Russian relations. This was a sign that Europe, not the empire, was now the focal point of British policy and that Germany, not Russia,was now the 'bogey-man'. He also tried to take a more tolerant view of Russia's aspirations in the Balkans, recognising that 'good relations with Russia meant that our old policy of closing the Straits', to her warships should end. This willingness to review the issue of the passage of Russian warships between the Black Sea and the Mediterranean made it easier for Izvolsky, the Russian foreign minister, to persuade his colleagues to accept the 1907 agreement.

* The strategic and economic importance of the Straits to Russia was steadily increasing in this period. To secure control over 'the keys and gates of the Russian house' was widely regarded as 'Russia's most important task in the 20th century'. So tempting a prize were they that Izvolsky was prepared to give a lot in return for international agreement to changing the Rule of the Straits of 1841, so as to allow Russian warships to pass from the Black Sea to the Mediterranean. In a rather impulsive and dangerous way, Izvolsky launched himself into unofficial talks with other European foreign ministers.

The Austro-Hungarian foreign minister, Aehrenthal, was quite receptive to the idea of a 'deal' since he was considering a project of his own in the Balkans – the annexation of Bosnia. The two became linked, creating the Bosnian Crisis of 1908–9, as it is called, which destroyed the Austro-Russian *détente* of 1897 and exacerbated existing problems in the Balkans. The 1897 agreement had put the Balkans 'on ice' for a decade. Instead of confrontation. Austria and Russia experimented with co-operation. However, Aehrenthal decided that the time had come to end the ambiguous status of Bosnia which, together with Herzegovina, had been 'administered' by Austria since the Congress of Berlin in 1878.

Austria's rights in these two provinces seemed in 1908 to be at risk. A new regime, the 'Young Turks' had just come to power in Constantinople, dedicated to the revival of the Ottoman Empire. Restoring Bosnia to full Turkish rule was one of their objectives. To prevent this, Austria decided formally to annex the provinces. This was meant to 'regularise' their status – to draw a clear line between what was Austrian territory and what was Turkish. The Turks, not surprisingly, saw it differently. To them it looked like seizure of a Turkish province and they demanded compensation for its loss. The annexation of Bosnia also angered Serbia because she regarded the Bosnian Serbs as belonging to a future Greater Serbia. Too weak to challenge the Austrians by herself, she looked to Russia for support.

˙* To the complexities of Balkan politics, however, was now added Izvolsky's unorthodox diplomacy. In return for Austria's acceptance of Russia's desire to control the Straits, he agreed in September 1908 to the annexation of Bosnia. This was a betrayal of Serbia, Russia's most recent client state in the Balkans. It was also hazardous because he acted without the knowledge of the prime minister. Izvolsky had only just begun to negotiate with the other powers over the issue when the Austrians announced the annexation of Bosnia in October 1908. When they rejected his demand for a European conference to discuss the problems, Izvolsky's scheme was in ruins and Russia was placed in a very embarrassing situation. Tension mounted when Serbia demanded compensation and threatened war. In January 1909, the German government decided that this was a favourable moment for Austria to smash Serbia while Russia was still too weak to face a war, so she promised Austria simultaneous mobilisation as a sign of her full support.

Neither France nor Britain showed any such support for Russia. They blamed Izvolsky for the crisis. Tension continued until late March, when Russia accepted Germany's 'ultimatum' that she recognise the annexation of Bosnia. Serbia, threatened with war by Austria, climbed down and agreed to 'live at peace' with Austria-Hungary.

The Bosnian crisis exacerbated Balkan problems and created much alarm in Europe. Russia felt humiliated, while Serbia was embittered, but not destroyed. It also revealed that the Triple Alliance was much more solid than the 'Triple Entente' of Russia, France and Britain. Above all, the crisis ended the Austro-Russian *détente* of 1897 over the Balkans.

* The years 1905 to 1909 saw a great increase in international tension. Germany's responsibility for this was considerable. She had provoked the Moroccan crisis, exploiting Russia's weakness to threaten France. Although not a prime mover in the opening of the Bosnian affair, she chose to back Austria to the hilt in January 1909, even though her ally had not consulted her about the annexation plan. Since Austria had turned a dubious bargain into a crisis on her own initiative, Germany was not committed. She could have exercised a moderating influence. Instead she chose the opposite path. Before the Bosnian crisis was over, Germany was involved in another source of tension in Europe – a naval race with Britain.

4 Naval Rivalry and the Agadir Crisis, 1908–12

In the winter of 1908–9 a 'naval scare' erupted in England through fear of Germany's expanding fleet. The launching in 1906 of the new all-big-gun battleship, called the *Dreadnought*, popularly believed to have made all existing battleships obsolete, was at the root of the alarm. Britain's massive lead in conventional warships seemingly no longer counted. By 1908 the damage done to Anglo-German relations made both governments consider proposals to reduce their building programmes, but nothing came of the talks that lasted from 1908 to 1912. British suspicions of Germany deepened further in 1911, when a second crisis arose over Morocco (the Agadir Crisis). Alarmed at how close to war they had been, the British government renewed its efforts for an Anglo-German understanding, but without success.

The prime objective of the Navy Laws of 1898 and 1900, prepared by Admiral von Tirpitz, was to create a powerful battle fleet of about sixty large warships by 1918, designed for operations in the North Sea. The German navy would have grown in size even if Tirpitz had not been appointed chief of the navy office in 1897. Navies were becoming status symbols and for many Germans naval expansion was a natural expression of their economic power and growing overseas trade. Tirpitz's battle fleet, however, was conceived as a 'power-political instrument' (not as a commerce-protection fleet) to be used either as a lever, or as a threat, to obtain colonial concessions from Britain. The objective of challenging Britain to secure what he called 'world political freedom' for Germany was implicit in the Tirpitz Plan from the outset. It was not made explicit for obvious reasons.

The plan suffered from several miscalculations. The British Admiralty, correctly diagnosing the potential threat, instituted countermeasures from 1902. The re-deployment of ships previously scattered across the globe concentrated a more powerful fleet in home waters and battleship construction was raised to four ships a year from 1905. A major reason for the navy scare of 1908–9 was the drastic reduction in this construction programme by the new Liberal government, elected in 1906, which wanted to reduce expenditure on armaments. The reduction also coincided with an increase in the German building tempo to four a ships a year. Hence the fear that by 1911 Germany could have thirteen Dreadnoughts to Britain's twelve. Yielding to pressure, the Liberal government reluctantly accepted the demand for no less than eight battleships in the naval estimates for 1909. The naval race was on!

In Britain, opponents of the naval race, including the pro-German members of the Cabinet, pressed for negotiations with Germany to reduce international tension. In Germany, both Bulow and his successor as Chancellor in 1909, Bethmann Hollweg, were alarmed at the strength of British hostility to Germany over the navy issue. But neither Wilhelm II nor Tirpitz was willing to make substantial concessions. For the Kaiser the navy was an obsession – it was 'his fleet' and he angrily rejected any interference with it or with his position as 'Supreme War Lord'. The most Tirpitz would agree to was a slackening of the tempo of construction, not a reduction in the size of the German fleet.

* Negotiations for a naval agreement began in 1909. In reply to Britain's proposals for naval reductions, the Chancellor offered a relaxation of tempo for three years linked to a political agreement. The neutrality agreement offered by Germany was a rather one-sided bargain. As Grey commented: 'It would separate us from Russia and France and leave us isolated.' From Germany's point of view, of course, that would be highly desirable. Further negotiations in 1910 foundered on the same rock.

The damage done to Anglo-German relations by the naval rivalry was immense. It crystallised, as no other issue could do, all the latent fears and suspicions of Germany's aims that had been aroused since the early 1900s. It also caught the attention of the press and public opinion much more forcefully than did other issues. A newspaper editor warned Germany in 1905, 'Any power which challenges Britain's supremacy offers her a menace, which she cannot ignore'. In similar vein, the foreign secretary insisted in 1913, 'The Navy is our one and only means of defence and our life depends upon it'.

Germany, by contrast, was first and foremost a continental power, whose security depended primarily on her army. When the leading military power became the second naval power in Europe, England's security was felt to be at risk. For the first time for almost half a century, Englishmen had to countenance the prospect of invasion. Hence the determination to maintain her naval supremacy regardless of cost. In German eyes, on the other hand, Britain's naval supremacy did not belong to her by some sort of 'divine right'. But it was disingenuous of German leaders, such as Tirpitz and the Kaiser, to pretend that their fleet programme was compatible with Anglo-German friendship. The effect of this naval rivalry in increasing the British government's suspicions of German aims was revealed during the Agadir Crisis.

* The Second Moroccan Crisis began in July 1911 when a German gunboat, the *Panther*, arrived at the Moroccan port of Agadir. The aim was to intimidate the French government into paying substantial territorial compensation in return for recognition of a French protectorate over Morocco. French troops had occupied the capital, Fez, in May, at the Sultan's request, following the outbreak of a revolt. This was widely regarded as prelude to a French take-over of Morocco. Although that would contravene the Algeçiras Act of 1906, Germany had disclaimed any political interest in Morocco in 1909 in

return for a sort of economic partnership agreement. The Germans, however, did have a justified grievance in that French officials were not honouring that agreement, by obstructing German economic activities in Morocco.

The crux of the dispute in 1911 was how much territorial compensation Germany could extract from France. Related to that was what degree of pressure was required to achieve it. There is no doubt that the German foreign minister, Kiderlen, grossly mishandled the situation. He attempted to pull off a 'great stroke' – impressing German public opinion by a prestige victory but at the same time winning French goodwill by accepting a protectorate over Morocco. But he set his target too high – demanding the whole of the French Congo – and conducted German diplomacy in an extremely provocative way. Neither the Chancellor nor the Kaiser shared his enthusiasm for 'thumping the table', as he put it.

The French government was conciliatory and prepared to pay what they considered a fair price for Germany's goodwill. Kiderlen, however, convinced himself that only threats would succeed: 'They must feel that we are prepared to go to the extreme,' he said.

By persisting throughout July in his demand for the whole of the French Congo, Kiderlen made a quick and amicable settlement impossible. His main miscalculation, however, was in not seeing that the unspoken threat to France could only succeed if Britain stayed out of the affair. But the British government, uneasy at the *Panther* incident, became alarmed after their enquiries to Berlin met with total silence. In late July, Lloyd George, a powerful Cabinet minister hitherto noted for his pro-German sentiments, gave a speech at the Mansion House in London which demonstrated that Britain had no intention of being ignored in any agreement over Morocco.

* After this speech the crisis took a new turn. What had begun as a Franco-German colonial squabble became a major Anglo-German confrontation. The British government was certainly over-reacting when the fleet was put on the alert and plans for British military assistance to France were finalised.

* It was a rather bizarre situation. As one historian has remarked, 'War between Great Britain and Germany stood clear on the horizon. Yet, oddly enough, war between France and Germany was never in sight'. A Franco-German accord was eventually signed in early November. Germany only obtained two meagre strips of territory in the French Congo – to the fury of German opinion which had been led to expect a great triumph of German diplomacy. Kiderlen's 'great stroke' had failed all round. He had not won popularity for the government and he had antagonised, not conciliated, France. An example, perhaps, of *Weltpolitik* at its worst – confusion of aims and heavy-handed methods, resulting in limited gains for Germany at the price of considerable tension.

In England, the risk of war during the Agadir Crisis revived the pressure for an Anglo-German *rapprochement*, but the mission of Lord Haldane, the war minister, to Berlin in February 1912 was not a success. The Germans repeated their demand for a neutrality pact, offering in exchange only a slower rate of warship construction.

Having failed to secure a naval limitation treaty with Germany, Britain negotiated a naval agreement with France in 1912–13. In essence, this made Britain responsible for the Channel while France was to guard the Mediterranean. Taken in conjunction with the 'military conversations' revived in 1911, Britain had made an extensive, albeit informal, commitment to the defence of France by 1913. Anglo-Russian naval talks were also held, in secret, in 1914 but no agreement had been reached by the outbreak of war.

5 The Balkan Wars, 1912–13

After the conclusion of the Bosnian crisis in 1909, the Balkans enjoyed a brief period of relative peace. This ended in 1911 when Italy, in pursuit of her ambitions in Tripoli (modern Libya) – then part of the Ottoman Empire – resorted to naval operations in Turkish waters, including an attack on the Dardanelles.

The revelation of Turkey's weakness in this conflict encouraged the expansionist ambitions of several Balkan states. In the First Balkan War of 1912 they defeated the Turks. The Second Balkan War arose in 1913 when the victors fell out amongst themselves. The main beneficiary of these wars was Serbia, which made large territorial gains. This was a disaster for Austria-Hungary because of Serbian support for the south Slavs who, by 1910, had created a radical protest movement uniting Serbs and Croats against Magyar domination in Hungary. For Austria-Hungary in particular, and for the great powers in general, the Balkan Wars were an unlooked-for and dangerous crisis, which they attempted to defuse by influencing the peace settlement in the interests of the Concert of Europe.

In the Spring of 1912 Serbia formed a Balkan Alliance with Bulgaria, to which Greece and Montenegro adhered in the autumn. Its main object was to free Macedonia of Turkish rule and divide it amongst the allies. Macedonia was roughly that third of the 'Big Bulgaria' (created by Russia in 1878 at the Treaty of San Stephano) which was returned to Turkish rule at the Congress of Berlin. Russian agents with strong Pan-Slavist sympathies played an important part in creating the Balkan Alliance. Despite this, the Russians were ill-informed about its real objectives and believed that its purpose was to resist the spread of Austrian influence. The Austrians also failed to grasp what was impending. Consequently, neither of them acted

The Balkan Wars, 1912–13

quickly enough to take effective measures against the threat to the status quo in the Balkans.

In two major battles, the Balkan League defeated the Turkish forces and subsequently crushed an attempted counterstrike. The peace treaty had only just been signed when Bulgaria, suspicious of Greek and Serb intentions, attacked Serbia. Routed by Greek and Serb forces, Bulgaria was obliged to surrender most of her gains from the First Balkan War.

The London Conference, which met after the First Balkan War, included representatives of the belligerent states and the ambassadors of the great powers. With both England and Germany playing a mediating role, Grey and the German ambassador were able to induce Russia and Austria-Hungary to give way on some crucial issues and to accept the need for compromises. Thanks to their mediation the most contentious questions were eventually resolved – though not without the threat of force at times. The main source of tension amongst the great powers was Austria-Hungary's determination to restrict Serbian territorial expansion, while Russia felt obliged to support her claims. Although the Austrians succeeded in their aim of creating an independent Albania (a non-Slav state), there was acute friction over its boundaries, especially the inclusion of the fortress town of Scutari.

  * The London Conference was widely regarded as a triumph for Grey's patient diplomacy. It was also a tribute to Anglo-German co-operation, when their own interests were not directly involved. The main dissentient from this view was the Austro-Hungarian foreign minister. Disenchanted by the 'horse-trading' that went on, he complained that questions were not decided on the merits of the case but on the basis of great power alignments. This was partly true. The Russians, however, complained that the concessions they made were not matched by the Austrians. More serious was the ineffectiveness of the Concert's pressure on recalcitrant states, such as Montenegro. The Austrians maintained that it was their threat to use force which secured Scutari for Albania in April 1913 and which ensured the evacuation of Serbian forces from Albanian territory in October. Austrian disenchantment with 'Concert Diplomacy' was a significant factor in 1914.

  * The outcome of the Second Balkan War was disastrous for Austrian interests. Serbia acquired even more territory in Macedonia while Bulgaria, Austria-Hungary's most reliable friend in the Balkans, was greatly weakened after her defeat by Serbia and Greece. Furthermore, because of rival territorial claims, it was impossible for Austria-Hungary to assist Bulgaria without offending Rumania, whose fidelity to her alliance with Austria-Hungary was already in doubt. The one consolation for Austria-Hungary was that the Kaiser eventually woke up to the realities of Balkan politics. In typically flamboyant

manner, he assured his ally, 'I am prepared to draw the sword whenever your moves make it necessary'.

Russia, by contrast, had done rather well out of the Balkan Wars at very little cost to herself. Serbia, described as 'practically speaking a Russian province', was much enlarged and now boasted an army of 200 000 men. Rumania was wavering in her alliance with Austria-Hungary while Bulgaria, her protégé, was weakened. In short, whereas Austria-Hungary had been the dominant power in the Balkans after the Bosnian crisis of 1908, the Balkan Wars of 1912–13 changed the situation in Russia's favour.

* From Europe's point of view, however, there were two disquieting aspects to Russian policy. The first was the impetuous behaviour of the Russian war minister who instituted partial mobilisation in December 1912, until overruled by the Tsar's Council of Ministers. Secondly, as Grey recognised, Russia seemed to have little control over her Balkan protégés. Serbian nationalism, especially in its expansionist Pan-Serb form, was an explosive force that could easily involve Russia in a confrontation with Austria. The Balkan Wars can therefore be viewed as constituting a major step towards the outbreak of war in 1914. A former Russian foreign minister, Izvolsky, predicted in 1912 that the defeat of Turkey would accentuate the historic clash between Slavdom and Germanism. In this event, he saw little hope of avoiding 'a great and decisive general European war'.

6 The July Crisis, 1914

On 28 June 1914, at Sarajevo in Bosnia, the heir to the Austro-Hungarian throne was assassinated by a member of a Serb terrorist group. For the next three weeks there was little indication, at least on the surface, that Europe was moving towards a major crisis. Then, on 23 July, Austria presented a severe ultimatum to Serbia with a 48-hour time limit. Thereafter, events followed at such speed that diplomacy had little chance to avert war. Even last-minute attempts by the Kaiser and others were of no avail. In the last days of July the influence of military leaders seemed greater than that of civilians in some states. By August 4, the great powers of Europe were at war.

The assassination of the Austrian Archduke, Franz Ferdinand, was not just the work of Serb or Bosnian terrorists. It was planned by a colonel of the Serbian General Staff who headed a nationalist movement, the 'Black Hand'. The complicity or connivance of Serb officials and the Serbian government is undeniable, as the Austrians suspected (but could not prove) at the time. The motive for the assassination is still not altogether clear. It may have been simply patriotic; it could have been intended to be provocative. It may also have been fear that the Archduke's plans to conciliate the south Slavs

would weaken the appeal of Serbian propaganda to the 4.5 million
Serbs and Croats within Austria-Hungary.

* The Austro-Hungarian foreign minister, Berchtold, agreed with
the Emperor that this latest Serbian affront to Austria-Hungary could
not be allowed to pass unpunished. In Berchtold's view it was a choice
between action or 'renunciation of our Great Power position'. Austria-
Hungary's prestige and survival demanded that severe reprisals be
taken to curtail Serbia's independence, even though this probably
meant war with Russia. Berchtold explained his views in these terms
on 21 July:

> 1 It was increasingly certain that the subversive activity pursued on
> Bosnian soil . . . and with ramifications in Dalmatia, Croatia,
> Slavonia and Hungary could be checked only by energetic action
> at Belgrade, where the threads run together; and that a new
> 5 grouping of Powers is coming into being in the Balkans with
> the connivance of Rumania and Russia, with the destruction of
> the Monarchy as its ultimate aim. . . . In drafting the note to Serbia
> it seemed to us essential, not only to document before the whole
> world our good right to put certain demands to Serbia for the
> 10 preservation of our internal tranquility; but to formulate these
> demands in such a way as would oblige Serbia to take up a clear
> position against propaganda hostile to the Monarchy, as regards
> the past and in the future, and as would give us a chance of
> making our voice heard in the matter in future. For us it was
> 15 not a question of humiliating Serbia, but of bringing about a
> clear situation regarding Serbia's relations with the Monarchy as
> a neighbour, and, as a practical result, either, in the event of
> our demands being accepted, a thorough clearing up of the
> situation in Serbia with our co-operation or, in the event of their
> 20 being refused, settling the matter by force of arms and paralysing
> Serbia as much as possible.

* If the Austrians had taken swift retaliatory action against
Serbia, a European war might have been averted. Although political
assassination was nothing new in 1914, many contemporaries, including
the Tsar, were shocked by the murder of the heir to the Habsburg
throne. Speed and efficiency were not, however, characteristics for
which Austria-Hungary was noted. A further impediment to prompt
action was the attitude of Tisza, the Hungarian prime minister, whose
assent was needed to important decisions affecting the Dual Monarchy.
He insisted on strict legality in the government's response to Sarajevo
and it was not until mid-July that Tisza finally consented to the
despatch of a severe ultimatum to the Serbian government. The chance
of a surprise move was therefore missed. Delivery of the Note to
Belgrade, the Serbian capital, was further delayed until the end of the
French President's visit to Russia on 23 July, in case his presence in

St Petersburg facilitated Franco-Russian solidarity. The ultimatum gave the Serbian government 48 hours to reply to the following terms:

1   The Royal Serbian Government will pledge itself to the following:
       1. to suppress every publication likely to inspire hatred and contempt against the Monarchy or whose general tendencies are directed against the integrity of the latter;
5   2. to begin immediately dissolving the society called the *Narodna odbrana* (Black Hand); to seize all its means of propaganda and to act in the same way against all the societies and associations in Serbia, which are busy with the propaganda against Austria-Hungary;
10   3. to eliminate without delay from public instruction everything that serves or might serve the propaganda against Austria-Hungary, both where teachers or books are concerned;
       4. to remove from military service and from the administration all officers and officials who are guilty of having taken part in
15   the propaganda against Austria-Hungary, whose names and the proofs of whose guilt the Imperial Government will communicate to the Royal Government;
       5. to consent that Imperial Officials assist in Serbia in the suppressing of the subversive movement directed against the
20   territorial integrity of the Monarchy.

The Austrian ultimatum shocked several foreign ministers by its severity, but the cleverly worded Serbian reply led many, including the Kaiser, to regard it as conciliatory. The real attitude of the Serbian government, however, was obscure since, while the reply actually rejected very little, it did not clearly accept very much of the ultimatum. Two factors seem to have influenced the decision not to accept the Note unequivocally. Firstly, the fear that the degree of complicity of the Serbian government would be revealed. The second was the assurances of support received from St Petersburg on 25 July. From this moment on there was almost no chance of the conflict being limited to Austria-Hungary and Serbia. At the least, Germany would be drawn in to defend her ally against a Russian attack.

The Kaiser's reaction to the Sarajevo murder was to insist that the Serbs be dealt with once and for all. At a meeting on 5 July it was decided to give complete support to Austria-Hungary even at the risk of war with Russia. This was the famous 'blank cheque', as it has been called. At the same time the Austrians were urged to 'act at once'.

*   In early July the German leaders thought that swift retaliatory action against the Serbs was necessary. Failure to act would undermine Austria-Hungary's credibility as a great power and reduce her value to Germany as an ally. It does seem, however, that Germany was in something of a dilemma. In Bethmann Hollweg's words, 'If we urge

them ahead, they will say we pushed them into it; if we dissuade them, then it will be a matter of leaving them in the lurch. Then they will turn to the Western Powers and we will lose our last ally'. At this time it also seemed quite possible, if not probable, that 'Russia was not at all ready for war.' As late as 18 July, the German foreign minister maintained: 'The more boldness Austria displays (and) the more strongly we support her, the more likely Russia is to keep quiet'. A week later, when it seemed clear that Russia would intervene, there was still the possibility that France would not support her in a Balkan squabble. In that case the Triple Entente would be shattered. Even if this gamble did not come off the German leaders felt they still had a good chance of winning a 'continental war' in 1914, when Russia's army reforms were not completed. German policy in the July crisis could therefore be regarded as a series of 'calculated risks' – but the risks were increasing at every stage. The alternative, however, seemed to be the decline of Austria-Hungary as a great power.

The Russian foreign minister was shocked by the terms of the Austrian ultimatum to Serbia on 24 July. 'This means a European war', Sazonov exclaimed. Misinformed about the involvement of the Serbian government, he interpreted Austria-Hungary's action as a deliberate provocation. This misjudgement was important because Sazonov might well have accepted a limited riposte against Belgrade if he had known the truth about Serbian involvement.

* The crucial decisions on which Russian policy was based for the remainder of the crisis were taken on 24–25 July. At the meeting of the Council of Ministers, Sazonov argued that Russia's conciliatory stance in earlier Balkan disputes had been interpreted by Germany as a sign of weakness. Russia's prestige with the Slav nations, as well as her influence in the Balkans, was at stake. In addition, German arrogance towards the Slavs was an affront to the dignity of Russia, the leading Slav state. In this crisis, therefore, Russia must stand firm – even at the risk of war. The government agreed to begin quite extensive preparatory military measures on 26 July and to proceed to partial mobilisation if Serbia were attacked.

July 27 should have been the day when Europe's leaders peered into the abyss and shrank back from the brink of war. The British foreign secretary, Grey, had been slow to grasp the gravity of the situation. Shocked into a sudden realisation of how serious the crisis had become by the Austrian ultimatum on 24 July, he despatched a series of desperate appeals to Berlin. His aim was to secure German participation in negotiations for a diplomatic solution to the crisis. Berlin not only rejected most of these appeals but pressed Austria to declare war on Serbia. This was done on 28 July. Belgrade was bombarded the next day by gunboats on the river Danube, even though the Austro-Hungarian army was not ready for action against Serbia for another two weeks.

★ Having escalated the crisis, Berlin showed signs of having second thoughts. By this time, however, events were beginning to move too fast for statesmen to control them. For example, the Kaiser insisted that Grey's final appeal should be acted on. Vienna was therefore asked to accept the Serbian reply (regarded as satisfactory by the Kaiser) as a basis for negotiations, and to 'Halt in Belgrade'. The Austrians, however, replied that it was too late. By late July military leaders were taking over the decision-making. Hence, on 28 July, Vienna received both the Kaiser's appeal for restraint as well as Moltke's demand for Austria's immediate mobilisation. This prompted the question from Berchtold: 'Who rules in Berlin – Moltke or Bethmann Hollweg?'

There has been some debate about Bethmann Hollweg's role in the later stages of the July crisis. His critics (especially Fischer) allege that he was less concerned with trying to avoid war than with creating favourable conditions for Germany to win it. On the other hand, it is arguable that Bethmann Hollweg could see no viable alternative to supporting Austria-Hungary and so believed that the decision for war or peace rested with Russia.

★ In Russia, full mobilisation was decreed on 30 July after several days of military preparations. Once Russia had mobilised, war could not be avoided. This was the legacy of the Schlieffen Plan which Moltke, the German Chief of Staff, inherited (and adapted) from his predecessor. As a solution to Germany's problem of fighting a war on two fronts, Schlieffen had planned a massive opening assault in the west with only a holding action on the eastern front. The plan sought to capitalise on Russia's notorious slowness in putting her vast armies into the field. By the time the Russian army was fully prepared for action, the main German army was supposed to have won a major victory over France. This was to be achieved by the sheer weight and speed of the attack. The modifications Moltke made to the original plan only increased the importance of speed, especially in the first few days of the war. For example, the Belgian fortress of Liège had to be seized on day 3 of mobilisation – a crucial fact kept secret from both the Chancellor and the Kaiser. Hence, whereas other European governments could honestly echo the French claim that 'Mobilisation is not war', Germany could not. Russia's mobilisation was therefore followed by Germany's mobilisation accompanied by a declaration of war on 1 August. Within two days, Germany had declared war on France and violated Belgian neutrality, as the Schlieffen Plan required. The Kaiser's attempt to re-direct the offensive eastwards was rejected because there were no plans in 1914 for fighting a war solely against Russia.

The violation of Belgium's neutrality, guaranteed by the powers in 1839, greatly influenced Britain's decision on 4 August to go to war against Germany. Whereas Grey insisted that Britain should support

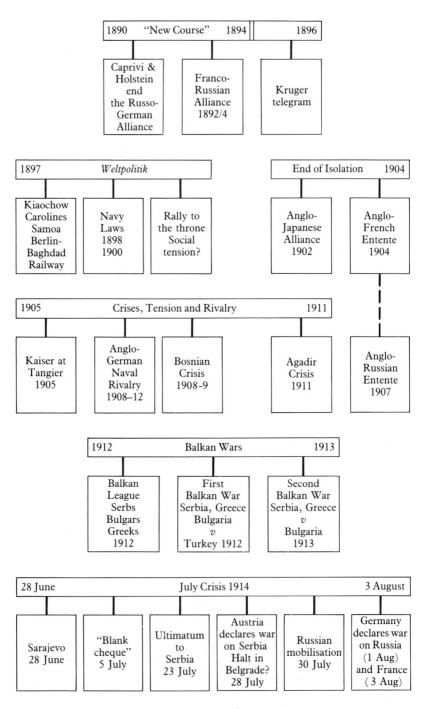

1890	"New Course"	1894		1896
Caprivi & Holstein end the Russo-German Alliance	Franco-Russian Alliance 1892/4		Kruger telegram	

1897	Weltpolitik		End of Isolation	1904
Kiaochow Carolines Samoa Berlin-Baghdad Railway	Navy Laws 1898 1900	Rally to the throne Social tension?	Anglo-Japanese Alliance 1902	Anglo-French Entente 1904

1905	Crises, Tension and Rivalry		1911	
Kaiser at Tangier 1905	Anglo-German Naval Rivalry 1908–12	Bosnian Crisis 1908-9	Agadir Crisis 1911	Anglo-Russian Entente 1907

1912	Balkan Wars	1913
Balkan League Serbs Bulgars Greeks 1912	First Balkan War Serbia, Greece Bulgaria v Turkey 1912	Second Balkan War Serbia, Greece v Bulgaria 1913

28 June	July Crisis 1914				3 August
Sarajevo 28 June	"Blank cheque" 5 July	Ultimatum to Serbia 23 July	Austria declares war on Serbia Halt in Belgrade? 28 July	Russian mobilisation 30 July	Germany declares war on Russia (1 Aug) and France (3 Aug)

Summary – Weltpolitik and the Drift to War, 1890–1914

France, at least half the Cabinet were opposed to British intervention in a continental conflict. It was not until 2 August that the Cabinet reluctantly agreed to fight if Belgium's neutrality was violated.

France, whose president and prime minister were literally at sea from 23 to 29 July, played a minor role in the unfolding of the crisis. The French ambassador at St Petersburg, on the other hand, assured the Russian government emphatically that it could rely on French aid against Germany. The French premier's attempt to delay Russia's mobilisation, for fear of provoking Germany, arrived too late. When Germany declared war on Russia, France had little choice but to support her ally.

To sum up, it is hard to avoid the conclusion that the main responsibility for the actual outbreak of war in 1914 (as distinct from the larger issue of war origins) seems to lie with Germany. She did not exercise the close control over her ally that the situation demanded. It is also difficult to find a single constructive move that Germany made throughout the July Crisis.

Making notes on '*Weltpolitik and The Drift to War, 1890–1914*'

As you read the chapter, try to identify the ways in which German policy contributed to the growth of international tension before 1914. Think particularly about the role of the Kaiser and the explanations of *Weltpolitik*. Which of them seems the more convincing? You should also regard this chapter as providing much of the evidence for the different explanations of the causes of the First World War which you will encounter in the next chapter. (There is quite a lot of detail in this chapter so try to concentrate on the most important events.) The following headings and sub-headings should help to guide your selection of topics for taking notes:

1. German foreign policy 1890–96
1.1. Caprivi and the 'New Course' 1890–94. What was new?
1.2. The significance for Germany of the Franco-Russian alliance
1.3. Foreign policy after Caprivi, 1894–96
1.4. Conclusion. Did Bismarck's fall make much difference to German policy?
2. *Weltpolitik* 1897–1904
2.1. The aims of *Weltpolitik*. How coherent were they?
2.2. Domestic influences
2.3. Alternative interpretations. Which view seems more plausible?
2.4. The Kaiser's influence on German policy
2.5. Bülow's opposition to an Anglo-German alliance
2.6. Conclusion: achievements of *Weltpolitik* by 1904. Compare Germany's situation in 1896 and 1904
3. Crises over Morocco and Bosnia

Answering essay questions on '*Weltpolitik* and the Drift to War, 1890–1914'

Many of the questions asked on the period 1890 to 1914 also relate to the causes of the First World War. They will be considered either after the next chapter (see p. 142) or in the subsequent section devoted to general questions covering the whole period 1871–1914 (see p. 144). The questions on this topic focus on the two main issues: the aims and methods of German foreign policy from about 1890 to 1914; and broader aspects of international affairs between these dates.

Study the following questions that have been arranged on the basis of these two issues:

1 Why were relations between Britain and Germany satisfactory in 1890 but unsatisfactory by 1914?
2 'From the time of Bismarck's fall until 1914, German foreign policy was frequently clumsy and often provocative.' Discuss this verdict.

3 What were the priorities in German foreign policy from about 1900 to 1914?

4 To what extent did internal disunity lead Germany to adopt the foreign policy which led to the First World War?

5 Did the accession of Kaiser Wilhelm II in 1888 mark a key point in the development of international relations?

6 Assess the significance of the Moroccan crises of 1905 and 1911.

7 Examine the validity of the statement that between 1904 and 1914 'Europe drifted unwittingly into war'.

8 Was Germany's fear of 'encirclement' between 1890 and 1914 justified?

The majority of the questions relate to German foreign policy itself or to the reaction of other great powers to it. Consequently five or six key factors could form the basis of an answer to most of these questions. The factors you choose might include: the aims and methods of *Weltpolitik*; the influence of the Kaiser on German policy; crises and tension from 1905 to 1913; and the nature of the Triple Entente. At this stage it would be useful to make a list of examples of each of the factors given above (with examples of other factors you have selected). Under the heading '*Weltpolitik*' you would probably include examples such as: overseas expansion; powerful navy; domestic tension; abrasive diplomacy.

Questions 1 to 3 are fairly straightforward. Make a list of five or six major aims of German foreign policy that you would use to answer question 3 (a 'direct' question) and arrange them in order of importance. What examples would you choose as 'evidence' to substantiate your list of aims? Make a second list of examples of clumsy diplomacy that would be appropriate to question 2 (a 'challenging statement' type of question). Can you think of any 'no' points? Now consider which of the points from the lists you have made for the first two questions would be appropriate for an answer to question 1 (a 'direct' question). For question 4, a 'to what extent' type, write down three points under each of the two headings 'internal disunity' and 'other factors'. Which seems the stronger argument?

Look now at questions 5 to 8. Except for question 7, they are all 'direct' questions, so for each you need a list of five or six paragraph points, backed by evidence. What additional factors would you use to supplement the points noted earlier about German foreign policy? For example, an answer to question 6 would normally include reference to Anglo-German relations and the closer ties between Britain and France. For question 8 you would need to consider whether the Triple Entente was an offensive or defensive grouping of powers. Question 7 (a 'challenging statement') requires you to argue a case *for* and *against* the assertion that Europe 'drifted' into war. Refer back to your list of factors for policies or methods that could be seen as causes of international tension. Make a list of paragraph points under two suitable headings (*for* and *against*). Which seems the stronger argument? Add to this the main point you would make in an introduction and conclusion.

You will find that many of the factors and points you have used for this section will help you to follow the arguments in the next chapter and deal with the questions that follow it.

Source-based questions on 'Weltpolitik and The Drift to War, 1890–1914'

1 German diplomacy, 1890–96
Read carefully the three extracts on pages 88–9 and 90. Answer the following questions:
a) What explanations does Salisbury suggest for the changes that came about in German foreign policy following the dismissal of Bismarck?
b) What is described, in the third extract, as being Caprivi's policy? Does the writer of the extract agree with Caprivi? Explain your answer.
c) The wording of the Kruger Telegram, the second extract, appears uncontroversial at first reading. Why did it provoke such an adverse reaction in Britain?
d) The third extract implies a reason for the change in policy, other than those contained in the first extract. What is it?
e) In what ways do the first and second extracts present i) a coherent, and ii) a contrasting picture of German foreign policy?

2 German colonial aspirations
Read carefully the three extracts from Müller and from the Crowe Memorandum, given on pages 92–93. Answer the following questions:
a) What possible explanations of German policy does Crowe give in the first extract from his Memorandum?
b) The extract from Müller suggests another possible explanation. What is it?
c) Which of the explanations contained in the first extract is supported in the third extract? Justify your answer.

3 Anglo-French co-operation
Read carefully the three extracts from Lansdowne and Grey, given on pages 101–103. Answer the following questions:
a) What does Lansdowne hint at, in the first extract, as being the Kaiser's real reason for engaging in the 'Tangier escapade'?

b) What policy does Lansdowne suggest, in the second extract, as a way of dealing with the problems caused by Germany?

c) What, in the third extract, did France want from Britain? How far was Grey able to meet the French wishes?

d) Based on evidence contained in the three extracts, assess the effect on British policy of German belligerence.

e) What evidence do the first two extracts contain about the character and attitudes of Lansdowne? In what ways were Lansdowne's attitudes different from Grey's?

4 The July Crisis, 1914

Read carefully the extracts from Berchtold and from the Ultimatum to Serbia, given on pages 114 and 115. Answer the following questions:

a) What was 'the Monarchy' referred to by Berchtold?

b) Why did 'the Monarchy' regard Serbia as a threat to its survival?

c) In your own words, explain Berchtold's aim in dealing with Serbia as he did.

d) Which of the demands made in the Ultimatum put into effect Berchtold's insistence that Serbia should 'give us a chance of making our voice heard in the matter in the future' (line 16)?

e) How far is it justifiable to claim that Serbia could only have accepted the Ultimatum if she had been prepared to surrender her independence?

f) How convincing is Berchtold's claim that 'for us it was not a question of humiliating Serbia' (line 17)? Use evidence from both extracts in your answer.

CHAPTER 5

The Origins of the First World War

1 The Debate on War Origins

The publication of James Joll's book *The Origins of the First World War* seventy years after the war began indicates how prolonged the debate on the origins of the war has been. The student of the First World War is confronted with a plethora of possible causes and a bewildering variety of interpretations. One reason for this is that each generation of historians looks at the problem from a different point in time as well as in the light of new evidence, so that their assessment of the responsibility for causing this cataclysmic event changes. It is noteworthy also that the question of responsibility for the war has not been solely one of academic interest but has had a political dimension to it. For example, in the 1920s and 1930s German historians were quite successful in their attempt to show that the charge of 'war guilt' laid upon Germany in 1919 at Versailles was unfair. After 1939, however, British historians naturally had cause to review the question of Germany's aggressive ambitions in 1914. More recently, in the 1960s, Fritz Fischer's renewal of the accusation of German responsibility for the war reopened the question of continuity in German expansionist aims from 1914 to the Nazi regime.

* The polarities of the debate on war origins can be summed up in two phrases: 'Germany willed the war' and 'The nations of Europe stumbled into war.' Between these two extremes is a broad central position that holds that while no one nation can be held entirely responsible for the war, some nations were more responsible than others.

A further clarification of the scope of the debate is made possible by distinguishing between 'man-made forces' (such as expansionist ambitions, war plans, calculated decisions and so on) and 'impersonal forces' (such as capitalism, international anarchy and alliances). Although it is also possible to attempt to distinguish between 'long term' and 'short term' causes of the war, some of the factors seem to belong (rather confusingly) to both categories. On the other hand, there is usually a rough correlation between the amount of emphasis a historian gives to man-made forces and his assessment of German culpability. Impersonal forces such as capitalism and imperialism are naturally stressed by Marxist historians, but historians of other persuasions usually discuss a broad range of these forces as well.

The limitation of impersonal forces is that they fail to explain why a particular war broke out at a particular time. They need therefore to be linked in some way with the man-made forces that do show how a diplomatic crisis became a European war. Joll's use of the phrase 'patterns of concentric circles', by which he links these impersonal forces to the July crisis, is a helpful approach to the problem. Thus Joll explains the outbreak of the war in terms of the decisions taken by the political leaders in 1914. But he also tries to show that those decisions were influenced by these impersonal forces, or factors, which may well have limited the options open to the decision-makers in 1914.

2 German Responsibility for the War

In considering the highly controversial issue of Germany's responsibility for the war, some historians have made a useful distinction between her contribution to the growth of international tension from about 1900 to 1913 and her role during the July crisis itself. Thus a traditional view holds that, 'All the governments were responsible for the tension which came to a head in July 1914. But they were not equally responsible for the fatal turn of events' – for which Germany was culpable. This view has been turned upside down by Hinsley, who has suggested that, 'The German government was primarily responsible for the pre-war tension – and was far more responsible for the war because of the decisions it took between 1904 and 1913 than on account of anything it did after Sarajevo'. The argument has been taken one stage further by the German historian Fischer, who holds Germany responsible for both. The aggressive pursuit of *Weltpolitik* he argues, soured international relations from 1897 to 1912 while its failure inspired a bid for world power through war in 1914.

* In the view of Fischer and his 'disciples', Germany willed the war in 1914 in order to realise expansionist ambitions and to resolve an acute domestic crisis. The overseas policy pursued by Germany since 1897 had failed to produce the desired results in the form of a central African empire. The Kaiser's regime had consequently not derived the much-needed boost to its prestige that *Weltpolitik* was supposed to provide. By 1912–13, he argues, a major domestic crisis existed in Germany. In the 1912 elections the socialists, the SPD, greatly increased their vote and became the largest party in the *Reichstag*. Their supposedly revolutionary aims made them seem to be a major threat to the Kaiser's government and to the ruling élite. The ruling classes believed, Fischer maintains, that the best way to safeguard their authority was by means of a 'brisk jolly war'.

In addition, he argues, many Germans had come to regard a conflict between Teutons and Slavs as inevitable, an aspect of the more general fear of 'encirclement' which existed in Germany after the formation of the Triple Entente in 1907. Time was not on Germany's side since

Russia's army reforms were expected to be completed in 1916–17, enabling her to exploit her massive superiority in numbers. Hence the German Chief of Staff believed in July 1914 that 'a moment so favourable from a military point of view might never occur again'. Moreover, Fischer asserts that the decision was taken in December 1912 that Germany should launch a war at the first favourable opportunity. Its main objective would be to achieve expansionist goals in Europe and overseas. Germany would expand her power base in Europe by annexing territory in the east and possibly in the west as well. This was the so-called *Mitteleuropa* programme which, it was felt, could no longer be realised by peaceful means. A successful war would also enable Germany to become a major colonial power in Africa by acquiring French and Belgian colonies – the *Mittelafrika* policy.

Since, in Fischer's view, Germany was intent on war, he is able to present her policy during the July crisis as consistent with that aim. Firstly, she put pressure on Austria-Hungary to retaliate against Serbia even if it meant a general war. This was the famous 'blank cheque' of July 5th when Austria-Hungary was assured that she 'could count on Germany's full support'. Secondly, the German Chancellor was not seeking a peaceful solution but was manoeuvring so as to create the most favourable situation for Germany to win the war. This meant seeking Britain's neutrality and presenting Russia as the aggressor. Finally, Fischer draws attention to the pressure of the military for a rapid transition from mobilisation to the declaration of war, thereby eliminating a last-minute diplomatic solution.

The emphasis that Fischer places on Germany's responsibility for causing the war in 1914 has been elaborated by a number of other writers, especially German historians, such as Geiss and Berghahn. The latter emphasises the undemocratic nature of the 'Prusso-German constitution' and the central importance of the domestic crisis in German policy-making, which is not unlike the concept of 'social imperialism'.

The merit of Fischer's views lies partly in the new evidence that he found to demonstrate Germany's expansionist aims in the period before 1914, drawing attention to aspects of German policy that had been neglected hitherto. The attraction of his interpretation is that it welds into a coherent whole the aims of German foreign policy from about 1897 and the growth of international tension up to 1913, as well as German policy during the July Crisis itself, establishing the links between them. Above all, perhaps, Fischer and his followers are able to explain why the war began, rather than just the circumstances in which key decisions were made.

Paradoxically, one of its strengths is possibly its major weakness. It portrays a regime intent on achieving certain defined objectives, pursuing a seemingly coherent policy, whereas for much of the period before 1914 German policy seems contradictory and lacking in clear aims. It may well be that the Fischer school has misrepresented the purpose that *Weltpolitik* was meant to fulfil, presenting it as a cure for all Germany's ills – a magic wand – when it was only intended to be a patriotic umbrella. There is also a fundamental methodological weakness in Fischer's case.

Fischer maintains that the German government launched a war in July/August 1914 in order to realise expansionist goals which were elaborated in a statement of war aims produced in September. He is therefore obliged to 'argue backwards', but the evidence is by no means conclusive that the German leaders held these expansionist aims before the 'September Programme' was compiled. There is also the problem that other states drew up ambitious war aims after the war had begun, but these aims are not regarded as explaining why such states went to war in 1914.

Fischer's assertion that the German government decided on war as early as December 1912 is also based on dubious evidence. The meeting at which this decision was taken was an irregular one, at which the Imperial Chancellor was not present, so its significance is hard to establish. It also seems to have had remarkably little influence on German policy in the following year.

The emphasis placed by the Fischer school on the central role of the domestic crisis in the decision to launch a war in 1914 is also seen by some historians as excessive. Clear links between the two have not been established while both Bülow and Bethmann Hollweg explicitly dismissed war as a solution to the socialist problem.

Finally, it has been pointed out that by focusing almost exclusively on decision-making in Berlin, the Fischer school have created a distorted picture of the diplomatic situation in July 1914 which needs to be corrected by examining policy-making in other European capitals during the crisis.

3 The Responsibility of Other Powers

Although there is no doubt that Austria-Hungary was under pressure from Germany to retaliate against Serbia in July 1914, there is much evidence to suggest that she needed no prompting from Berlin to respond to the Sarajevo incident. What she did need from Germany was a promise of full support, if action against Serbia led to war with Russia.

Sarajevo presented Austria-Hungary with a basic dilemma. Inaction meant 'the renunciation of our Great Power position', as the foreign minister put it. Action against Serbia, however, would probably result in war with Russia. The stark choice seemed to be between the decline and disintegration of the empire and the risk of defeat in war. With

German support, however, the chances of defeat would be greatly reduced. In the view of the Emperor, Franz Joseph, Serbian support for the south Slav movement within the empire was provocation enough. After Sarajevo, it was necessary 'to eliminate Serbia as a political factor in the Balkans'.

It is sometimes argued that the Austrians opted for war in 1914 as an escape from the insoluble problem of conflicts between the various nationalities within the Habsburg monarchy. But according to F R Bridge, domestic chaos had become an occupational disease in Austria-Hungary; something one learned to live with, summed up in the phrase, 'The situation is hopeless, but not serious'. The real threat to the survival of the state in 1914 came from outside rather than from within.

* It is also arguable that Austria-Hungary contributed greatly to the development of the July Crisis by the lengthy delays in responding to Sarajevo. Had the Austrians presented Europe with a *fait accompli* by a rapid punitive strike against the Serbian capital, Belgrade, the outcome could well have been quite different. But, as the German Chancellor complained, 'They seem to need an eternity to mobilise'. The German government constantly pressed their ally to act quickly, largely in the hope that prompt action would permit the conflict to be kept localised. But the ultimatum to Serbia was not delivered until almost a month after Sarajevo.

A further way in which Vienna was responsible for the escalation of the crisis was that her declaration of war on Serbia on 28 July came only five days after the delivery of the ultimatum, which itself had a time limit of a mere 48 hours. Similarly, she would not halt her military operations, as the Kaiser suggested, even though negotiations with Russia were scheduled for 30 July. On a number of counts, therefore, Austria-Hungary contributed to the escalation of a major diplomatic crisis into a European war. This conclusion is only of significance, of course, if it is believed that Germany was anxious to keep the conflict localised. If the view is held that Germany was intent on a general war from the outset, then what the Austrians did in the course of the crisis is obviously of much less importance.

* Russia's responsibility for the outbreak of war in 1914 is seen as directly related both to her policy in the Balkans before 1914 and the decisions she took during the July Crisis itself. Historians such as Turner and Remak regard Russian policy as quite provocative. In the first place it seems clear that Russia was the expansionist force in the Balkans, not Austria-Hungary. Secondly, she was unable – and perhaps unwilling – to restrain or control Slav nationalism even though it was an explosive force, endangering peace and stability in Europe. In the course of the Balkan Wars, regarded by some historians as 'a Russian war which she fought by proxy' (through the Balkan League), the Russian high command pressed for mobilisation. In late July 1914,

Russia was the first of the great powers to mobilise, despite the implications of this, especially for Germany. Russia's promises of support for Serbia are believed to have influenced the decision not to accept the Austrian ultimatum, leading to the Austrian declaration of war. It is clear that Russia's prestige as a Balkan power and as a protector of the Slavs was at stake in 1914 but not her survival, as in the case of Austria-Hungary.

   * France and Britain are regarded by most historians as not playing a crucial role in the origins of the war. A form of 'nationalist revival' took place in France after 1911 but this represented a stiffening of morale rather than an aggressive anti-German stance. In 1912, France appears to have given a sort of 'blank cheque' to Russia by promising French support under any circumstances. This pledge was renewed in 1914 but this time it seems to have been the work of her ambassador in St Petersburg rather than official policy from Paris. Hopes of recovering Alsace-Lorraine gave France something worth fighting for, but not a sufficient reason for wanting war. Although Britain had no desire for war, her foreign minister seriously underestimated the gravity of the crisis in late July. It is possible that a clearer and prompter statement of British intent to support France might have exercised a restraining influence on Berlin. Some historians also suggest that Britain could have exerted more restraint on St Petersburg. The most serious charge against Britain, however, is that her naval talks with Russia in 1914 convinced the German Chancellor that the ring of encirclement around her was now complete. Grey's false denial of these secret talks also destroyed his credibility as a mediator in German eyes in the July crisis.

   Although the 'Fischer thesis' – that Germany willed the war in 1914 – has had an enormous impact on historical opinion in the last twenty years, many historians do not accept its exclusive emphasis on Germany's responsibility or the motives alleged for it. The real issue in 1914, they believe, was not a bid for world domination or a major domestic crisis but the desperate need to preserve Austria-Hungary's position as a great power and ally. The charge against Germany is that she pursued in an aggressive way what was an essentially defensive posture. In particular, she did not make a single constructive move in July to defuse the crisis but took a number of calculated risks, 'a series of gambles that did not work out', as Remak puts it.

4 The Balkans

Balkan problems have naturally long been regarded as a major factor in the origins of the First World War. The fundamental question, however, that has to be asked about the significance of the Balkan situation is whether it was the cause, or merely the occasion, of the war in 1914.

If Fischer is correct in asserting that Germany decided in December 1912 to launch a war at the first favourable opportunity, then the Sarajevo murder provided her with just the excuse for war that she wanted. It was an issue that deeply concerned her ally, unlike Franco-German quarrels over Morocco. It was also an issue that was readily intelligible to German public opinion, in contrast to the confusing conflicts of the Balkan Wars over remote places such as Scutari.

On the other hand, those historians who do not accept Fischer's view of Germany's motives in 1914 continue to regard Balkan problems as playing an important part in the origins of the war. This more conventional approach recognises the existence of both long and short term factors in the Balkan situation. It also regards nationalism in the Balkan states as an important example of the aggressive tendency of European nationalism in general by 1914.

The fate of the Ottoman Empire in Europe concerned the great powers for most of the nineteenth century. By the 1900s, however, Britain was no longer obsessed with the fear of Russia taking Constantinople and was prepared to discuss the issue of the Straits, especially after the signing of the *Entente* in 1907. On the other hand, the old tension between Austria-Hungary and Russia in the Balkans, evident in the crises over Bulgaria during the 1870s and 1880s, was renewed quite sharply, after a ten year respite (1897–1907), by the Bosnian Crisis of 1908–9 and the Balkan Wars of 1912–13. From the Austrian point of view, a Russian predominance in the Balkans would endanger her economic and political interests in the area. Since this was the only region where Austria-Hungary did exercise much influence, a threat to her prestige in the Balkans was all the more serious. Her status as a great power was dependent on it.

In the early 20th century, the crucial issue was the conflict between Austria-Hungary and Serbia. Serbian nationalism, an expansive force seeking to unite all Serbs into a Greater Serbia, was a deadly threat to the multinational Habsburg empire. Serbia's sense of grievance at the Austrian annexation of Bosnia, which had a large Serb population, was matched by Austrian alarm at Serbia's territorial expansion as a result of the Balkan Wars.

Russian patronage of Serbia dated from the early 1900s when the pro-Austrian ruling family was overthrown and Serbia ceased to be a sort of Austrian satellite. Russian support for the Serbs – an aspect of Pan-Slavism – was natural enough, but it was a highly dangerous development. Two of the great powers were now involved with the fate of one of the Balkan states. To add to the dangers, Russian influence over Serbia was limited, a situation aggravated by the fact that the Serbian government's control over nationalistic secret societies and the army was inadequate. In 1914 both Austria-Hungary and

Serbia engaged in 'brinkmanship', displaying great recklessness in a tense situation. In the view of some historians, the critical decisions were taken by them, rather than by Germany or Russia. In this sense, the 1914 war might be considered as the 'Third Balkan War'.

5 Alliances, International Anarchy and Armaments

Important though Balkan problems were in creating tension amongst the powers, leading to a crisis in 1914, they do not of themselves explain how an Austro-Serb dispute escalated into a general European war. Similarly, the existence of alliances does not explain why war broke out in 1914 but it does help to explain why so many powers became involved in it. The alliance system can therefore be regarded as one of several factors that contributed to the breakdown of peace, part of the 'pattern of concentric circles' of causal factors that limited the options available to statesmen in the July Crisis. The alliance system can also be seen to have had both long-term and short-term effects on international relations.

At first sight the short-term impact could be regarded as of great importance in 1914. Was it not the alliance system that dictated that Germany should support Austria-Hungary and France support Russia? An examination of these alliances, however, over a longer timespan suggests that significant changes had been introduced in their nature. The Austro-German Alliance had been used by Bismarck to restrain the activities of Austria-Hungary in the Balkans. For fifteen years after his downfall, this alliance had not played a very prominent part in international affairs. It was only in 1906, after her isolation at the Algeçiras conference, that Germany fully realised that Austria-Hungary was virtually her only ally and must therefore be preserved at all costs. This attitude was clearly demonstrated in the 'blank cheque' to the Austrians in early July 1914. What had been a defensive alliance was thereby almost converted into an offensive one, enabling the Austrians to retaliate against Serbia, even at the risk of war with Russia. But the blank cheque was not issued from an automatic dispenser. It was a deliberate decision taken in 1914 by Germany, whose obligations were to assist her ally if she were attacked by Russia. That the Austrians did not assume they could use the alliance for offensive purposes in 1914 is shown by the despatch of a special emissary to Berlin to sound out Germany's views.

* In 1914 France was obliged by the terms of the alliance to aid Russia once Austria-Hungary had mobilised. But in a similar way, it is argued, France had given her defensive alliance with Russia an offensive nature in 1912 by the promise of support under any circumstances – a French 'blank cheque' to Russia. It could be argued therefore that the crucial point in 1914 was not the existence of alliance systems but the fact that their former defensive nature had been altered.

One of the most important effects of the alliance system was to reduce the flexibility of the great powers' response to crises. The most obvious and possibly most important example of this was the impact of the Franco-Russian Alliance on German military planning in the form of the Schlieffen Plan. Germany's lack of a flexible response ensured that her reply to a threat from Russia was to invade France! When the Kaiser suggested in late July that German armies should attack in the east he was informed that it was logistically impossible.

On the other hand, it is possible to exaggerate the influence and the rigidity of the alliance system both during the July Crisis and before it. Italy, when the crisis came, refused to support her allies in the Triple Alliance, while Britain rejected appeals from her partners in the Triple Entente to make plain her intent to support them. The British government had still not decided to aid France by the end of July 1914. Between 1908 and 1913, moreover, the alliance system was far from rigid. Both Russia and Austria-Hungary expressed disappointment with the support received from their allies in Balkan affairs, while France derived little sympathy from Russia in her dispute with Germany over Morocco in 1911. Britain was also becoming increasingly disenchanted with Russia's blatant disregard for the agreement reached in 1907 over Persia. In a number of respects, therefore, the alliance system was in some disarray in early 1914.

Alliances can be seen as both a reflection of insecurity and a contribution towards it. French fears of Germany led her to seek an alliance with Russia. The conclusion of the Franco-Russian Alliance, however, increased Germany's sense of insecurity. This was intensified by Britain's agreements with France and Russia in 1904 and 1907, creating what the Germans called 'encirclement' but which Britain and her partners regarded as 'containment' of an unpredictable Germany.

  * The alliance system represented an aspect of what was often called 'international anarchy' which, it was said, turned Europe into a powder magazine needing only a spark to ignite it. The existence of sovereign states pursuing their own national interests in a highly competitive situation was bound, it was argued, to lead to war sooner or later. It is clear that the explanatory power of such observations is rather limited. Why, for example, did the war come later rather than sooner? Critics of the concept also point out that this so-called 'international anarchy' had been a fact of life in European affairs since at least 1870, during which time Europe had enjoyed over forty years of peace. Furthermore, the alliance system could be viewed as a restraining influence on the policies of sovereign states, constituting an aspect of the balance of power, as is shown by this extract from an editorial in The Times of April 1914:

1   The division of the Great Powers into two well-balanced groups
    with intimate relations between the members of each, which do
    not forbid any such member from being on the friendliest terms
    with one or more members of the other, is a twofold check upon
5   inordinate ambitions or sudden outbreak of race hatred.

The outbreak of war in 1914 shows that the balance of power did
not operate at all times in favour of peace. Alternatively, it may be
that, as A J P Taylor suggests, the war was caused by its breakdown
rather than by its existence. The balance of power had been upset by
the revelation of Russia's weakness in 1905, when defeat in the Far
East was followed by revolution at home. But Taylor's argument
suffers from the fact that war did not occur in 1905, but in 1914, by
which time Russia had recovered her strength. It might be more
logical, therefore, to suggest that the war resulted from Germany's
determination to alter the existing balance in her favour either in an
expansionist, offensive sense or as a defensive reaction to encirclement
and the recovery of Russian power.

   * Some historians see the outbreak of war as stemming from the
collapse of the Concert of Europe in the sense that some powers were
no longer willing to exercise restraint in the interests of 'Europe' as
a whole. Yet the Concert had operated successfully in dealing with
crises in the Near East in the 1870s and 1880s and had played a
crucial role in preventing war amongst the powers during the Balkan
Wars as recently as 1912–13. Why then did it fail to operate a short
while later in July 1914?

   One obvious answer is that Germany was intent on war in 1914,
whereas she had not been so minded in 1912–13. There was certainly
no shortage of mediation proposals in 1914, including a conference of
ambassadors – a device that had produced results on previous occasions.
But the German government rejected all but the last of these proposals.
The reason, however, for her refusals may have been less her own
wish for war than her desire to shield Austria-Hungary from the sort
of compromises that such conferences often resulted in. The German
Chancellor made the point explicitly in his reply to Grey's proposal
in late July for an ambassadorial conference when he said: 'Germany
could not bring Austria-Hungary's dealings before a European
tribunal'. The Austrian foreign minister made no secret of his
disillusionment with the way the Concert had operated during the
Balkan Wars and would have no truck with 'worthless face-saving
formulas' in 1914.

   A further argument of some force links German military planning
with the breakdown of concert diplomacy. The German government
could not tolerate a diplomatic defeat for her ally – but this might
well be the outcome of a great power conference. But, if the Russian
army was mobilised on Germany's eastern frontier while the conference

met, it would be impossible for Germany to reject the conference's findings even if they were unacceptable to Austria-Hungary. This was because Germany's chance of victory depended on surprise and speed. Without the vital weeks that Russia's cumbersome mobilisation process required, the Schlieffen Plan was doomed. Consequently, Germany might well have to accept whatever diplomatic solution Russia and France dictated. Faced with the possibility of a colossal diplomatic defeat for Austria-Hungary, Germany opted for war.

   * An arms race can be both a cause and effect of international tension. It is clear that in the years after about 1905 governments were reacting to the military and naval preparations of their neighbours. Attempts to reduce the level of armaments through disarmament conferences at the Hague in 1898 and 1907 were unsuccessful. If Germany made no secret of her hostility to such proposals, the delegates from most of the leading states were sceptical of their feasibility. With regard to land forces, there is not much sign of an arms race developing before about 1912. France actually reduced her period of service to two years in 1905, conscripting 250 000 men each year. The German total was slightly higher but well below the Russian figure of 330 000 while the Austrians conscripted less than half the French figure. Germany was spending so heavily on her naval programme after 1900 that there was little to spare for increases in her army.

   Before 1912, the arms race that attracted most attention was the Anglo-German naval rivalry. This undoubtedly poisoned relations between the two countries because of the threat posed to Britain's security from the determination of a great military power to create a formidable navy. In both countries the rivalry influenced the outlook not only of the naval authorities and the governments but also of public opinion. Britain's willingness to go to war in 1914 owed a lot to the anti-German feelings generated by the naval race.

   Although Germany, Austria-Hungary and France all increased the size of their peacetime armies between 1912 and 1914, so creating an arms race atmosphere, the main increase in army strength after 1905 took place in Russia. Her defeat in the Russo-Japanese war underlined the need for a drastic reorganisation of her armed forces, but the sheer size of the planned increase from 1.5 to 2.0 million was daunting. In Germany particularly, the Russian army reforms, due to be completed by 1917, caused immense anxiety. As Moltke put it in July 1914: 'Any delay reduces our chances, for we cannot compete with Russia when it is a question of masses.' From the point of view of the German high command, a preventive war against Russia in 1914 made sense.

   It is easier to see the force of a specific example such as this than to judge the validity of the general proposition that arms races inevitably lead to war. Although this was a widely held view in the

1920s and 1930s – hence the popularity of disarmament talks – the proposition is not readily susceptible to proof on the basis of historical evidence. For example, it is not usually argued that the Second World War was caused by an arms race. There is a more obvious case that the arms race contributed to a widespread feeling in 1914 that war could not be postponed indefinitely.

The existence of militarism in continental Europe exerted some influence on the decision for war in 1914. All the leading states had powerful armies, their governments mostly encouraged warlike attitudes and in some cases, notably Germany, the General Staff exercised enormous influence over the monarch and the government. Against this, however, has to be set the existence of quite powerful currents of anti-militarism in both France and Germany, especially amongst the socialist movements.

Most historians accept that the arms race increased international tension and heightened chauvinistic feelings amongst the public in general before 1914. It is also agreed that in some states the General Staff exercised so much pressure for mobilisation that diplomats found they had little freedom of manoeuvre as the crisis deepened in late July. The fact remains, however, that some governments were more willing than others to start a war in 1914 and the reasons were political, not military.

6 Capitalism, Imperialism and Nationalism

The role of impersonal forces such as imperialism in the origins of the war has long been controversial. It is clear that such forces cannot explain why a particular war broke out at a given moment in time, but they may constitute important underlying causes for war.

Some historians accept as axiomatic Marx's dictum: 'Wars are inherent in the nature of capitalism; they will only cease when the capitalist economy is abolished'. Capitalism was said to make war inevitable on two grounds, at least. Firstly, the rather simple belief that industrialists, especially armaments manufacturers, had a vested interest in provoking war to increase their profits or to ruin their competitors. Secondly, there was the more complex view that stressed the importance of capitalist economic pressures as the driving force behind the imperialist rivalries, which were said to be the main cause of the 1914 war.

Arguments such as these have the merit of simplicity but they do not necessarily take into account some of the complexities of the world of international trade and finance. A difficulty that arises is that it is easier to make generalisations such as, for example, that 'wicked capitalists' were, almost by definition, 'warmongers' than to demonstrate from the evidence of specific examples that the contrary was often the case. Clearly, armaments manufacturers such as Krupp or Vickers-Armstrong, the so-called 'merchants of death', profited from government armaments programmes in peacetime, but even they also had markets overseas which might be lost in wartime. Much the same could be said of steel manufacturers, with the added proviso that theirs was a complex trade, in which a variety of types and grades of steel were produced for different markets, at home and abroad. International bankers also had close contacts with politicians but their best interests were served by political stability. Although loans played a significant role in creating or reinforcing political ties between European states, financiers were not likely to favour crises which could put their investments at risk. In July 1914, there were fears in London of a complete financial collapse if Britain became involved in war.

* Anglo-German trade rivalry has been cited in particular as an example of capitalist competition leading to war. There were certainly complaints of unfair competition and loss of markets but these were mostly in the 1890s, before the trade revival took effect, or stemmed from trades which were particularly badly hit by German competition. In general, Britain's commercial links with Germany were growing closer from 1904 to 1914, with both sides establishing valuable markets in the other country and creating greater interdependence in manufacturing processes. Grey commented in 1906 that 'The economic rivalry (and all that) do not give much offence to our people, and they admire her steady industry and genius for organisation. But they do resent mischief making'. In short, economic considerations were not the main determinant of Anglo-German relations nor in the forefront of decision-making in July 1914.

* A connection between imperialism and war may seem more plausible than the link with capitalism, if only because imperialism had so many facets to it. Lenin, in particular, made a direct causal link between imperialism (itself a manifestation of capitalism) and war, arguing in 1916 that the war being fought amongst the great powers was an 'imperialist war', to effect a re-division of colonial territories.

Since Germany had a prime interest in acquiring the colonies of other states, this could explain her decision for war in 1914. Indeed, such a suggestion might seem to be in line with Fischer's argument that *Mittelafrika* was one of the key objectives of *Weltpolitik*. Two objections can be raised to this. Firstly, Fischer himself argues that by about 1912–13 the German government had switched its sights to the *Mitteleuropa* programme. Secondly, Germany's ambitions in Africa seemed to be realisable by peaceful negotiation with Britain. A more general connection between imperialism and great power conflict emphasising rivalry for concessions, loans and monopolies was asserted by other writers of this period, such as Brailsford, a Liberal of the Hobson mould.

* The political aspects of imperialism are regarded by historians such as Joll as having a more significant bearing on the origins of the war. It is indisputable that imperial rivalries created much hostility among the powers, as shown by the Franco-German clashes over Morocco. German *Weltpolitik* represented a serious challenge to the British Empire in general. Even so, agreements were being made on colonial issues in the years prior to the war, such as the Anglo-German negotiations on Africa in 1912–13. Moreover, the fact that Britain's imperial rivalries with France and Russia were resolved by the *ententes* of 1904 and 1907 makes general assertions about such rivalries leading to war seem untenable. On the other hand, the psychological consequences of a generation of imperialism, especially in terms of exacerbating mutual suspicion and hostility, contributed to the mood of 1914.

Imperialism also aroused nationalistic feelings in some of the European states, contributing to the so-called 'nationalist revival' in France following the Agadir Crisis of 1911. Nationalism itself had become a more aggressive force in many of the major states by the turn of the century. This trend was fostered by the popular press and by right wing pressure groups such as the Pan-German League and *Action Française*. A crude form of Social Darwinism inspired some, though not all, of these movements where a vigorous assertion of national interests was deemed a sign of the nation's health and vitality. The theme 'expand or decline' provided Pan-Germans with an expansionist programme at the expense of other states that was seemingly justified by the laws of nature.

Expansionist ambitions were not confined to Pan-Germans. Pan-Slavism was in some respects a cloak for Russian ambitions in the Balkans. Nor was it limited to the great powers. Pan-Serbism was only one form of Balkan nationalism. What made it so deadly was its direct challenge to the survival of Austria-Hungary. An older generation of historians certainly believed that the primary cause of the war in 1914 was the fact that political frontiers did not correspond to national groupings.

7 Conclusion

The immediate causes of the outbreak of war in 1914 are to be found in the July Crisis. Even so, the crucial decisions taken by the leading figures can be explained as either defensive or offensive in intent. These decisions were themselves influenced by the rise in international tension from about 1905, which was generated partly by German

Weltpolitik, partly by the revival of Balkan crises. Further complexity inevitably arises from an examination of the broader political and economic context in which great power diplomacy operated. This involves consideration of the more 'impersonal forces'; alliances, international anarchy, nationalism, imperialism and capitalism.

Some historians, however, might well insist that these forces were the real causes of the war and that the July Crisis was merely the inevitable manifestation of them. Others would more readily subscribe to Joll's concept of 'concentric circles', in which earlier situations and policies, together with impersonal forces, contributed to the frame of mind in which decisions were taken in 1914.

The complexity of the debate on war origins indicates that a mono-causal explanation of the 1914 war is not likely to be very convincing. It is possible, however, to identify a number of key factors, relegating others to a subsidiary role, even though this may be a very subjective process – a matter of opinion. There are, perhaps, four factors that could be regarded as central to an explanation of the 1914 war. They are: the legacy of *Weltpolitik*; the growth of Russian power; the disruptive effect of nationalism in southeast Europe; and the inadequacies of German policy during the July Crisis.

The legacy of *Weltpolitik* was twofold. Not only had it 'failed' by 1914, but it had also harmed Germany's relations with other powers. Its failure led to a sense of frustration amongst the country's leaders and public opinion at the meagre achievements (apart from the big navy) of the era of world policy, especially when contrasted with the high expectations held of it. Germany's overseas empire, for example, was not much bigger in 1914 than it had been in 1896. Germans could justifiably feel that they had not attained that position in world affairs to which their economic strength entitled them. An unexpected effect of *Weltpolitik* was to increase Germany's feeling of insecurity through a sense of 'encirclement' by hostile powers, following Britain's association with France and Russia in the so-called Triple Entente. But it was mainly the objectives and/or methods of German policy in the years after 1905 – for example, the naval race, the crises over Morocco and Bosnia and German expansion into the Near East – that had produced this alignment and given it an anti-German direction. Germany had good reason to feel much less secure by 1914 than in 1900, but it is hard to avoid the conclusion that this situation was largely of her own making.

The growth of Russian power in the decade before 1914, on the other hand, was a development that Germany could do nothing about. It was not just the implications of continuing economic expansion and population growth that alarmed Germany, but also Russia's army reforms and strategic railways, close to the borders with Germany. By 1916–17, the Germans believed, the Russian army would be a very formidable opponent. As A J P Taylor has pointed out: 'Where most of Europe felt overshadowed by Germany, she saw the more distant Russian shadow.'

If Russia's military recovery after 1905 meant that 1914 was Germany's 'last chance', Sarajevo was the 'last straw' as far as Austria-Hungary was concerned. The disruptive force of nationalism in south east Europe affected her in two ways. Firstly, conflicts between the nationalities within Austria-Hungary threatened the state with dislocation, weakening her ability to act as a great power. Secondly, the appeal of a Great Serbia to Serbs and Croats inside the Dual Monarchy threatened Austria-Hungary with disintegration. Serbia's assertive nationalism was a challenge that Austria-Hungary could not ignore, if she were to survive as a great power.

Finally, it can be argued that German policy after the murder at Sarajevo was inadequately conceived to meet the gravity of the situation. Taking a 'calculated risk' in encouraging the Austrians to retaliate against Serbia, in the hope of splitting the Triple Entente, was not altogether reckless. It was possible that Britain and/or France might fail to give Russia firm support over yet another unwanted crisis in the Balkans. This would result in a weakening of the Entente, thus breaking the nightmare of 'encirclement'. The culpability of the German leaders lay in their failure to devise 'contingency plans', or diplomatic alternatives, if the initial gamble on French or British indifference to another Balkan crisis failed. The inadequacies of German policy – assuming she was not intent on a general war – could be regarded as a crucial factor in converting a diplomatic crisis into war. In view of the impact of *Weltpolitik* on international relations and of Germany's role in the July Crisis, it seems fairly clear that Germany's responsibility for causing the war was greater than that of any other power.

A number of other factors can be considered to have played a subsidiary role in the origins of the war. The selection of these is, once again, somewhat arbitrary and very much a matter of opinion. Four such factors might be: the decline of the 'Concert'; the armaments race; the legacy of imperial rivalries; and the influence of domestic tensions on foreign policy decisions.

It is clear that in 1914 the destructive capacity of modern European states greatly exceeded their ability to adopt a constructive approach towards solving a serious crisis. Yet some mechanism was needed in 1914 to moderate the pursuit of national self-interest as the main determinant of foreign policy. The 'Concert of Europe' had fulfilled this function in the 19th century, but in 1914 some statesmen were unwilling to behave with restraint for the sake of 'Europe' as a whole. Secondly, the arms race not only increased expectations of war but also led Germany to believe that she had a better chance of winning a land war in 1914 than in a few years' time. Thirdly, the imperialist rivalries of previous decades had increased animosities among the great

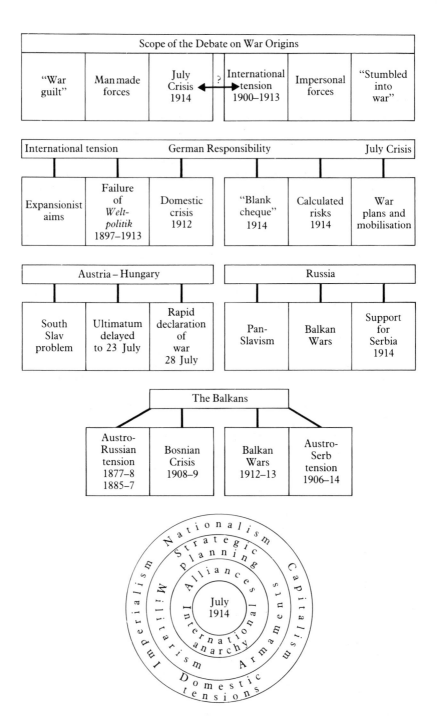

Scope of the Debate on War Origins					
"War guilt"	Man made forces	July Crisis 1914	? International tension 1900–1913	Impersonal forces	"Stumbled into war"

International tension		German Responsibility			July Crisis
Expansionist aims	Failure of *Welt-politik* 1897–1913	Domestic crisis 1912	"Blank cheque" 1914	Calculated risks 1914	War plans and mobilisation

Austria – Hungary			Russia		
South Slav problem	Ultimatum delayed to 23 July	Rapid declaration of war 28 July	Pan-Slavism	Balkan Wars	Support for Serbia 1914

The Balkans			
Austro-Russian tension 1877–8 1885–7	Bosnian Crisis 1908–9	Balkan Wars 1912–13	Austro-Serb tension 1906–14

Summary – The Origins of the First World War

powers, affecting the attitudes not just of governments but also of public opinion and the press, contributing to the warlike mood of July 1914. Finally, the existence of domestic tensions in countries such as Germany, Austria-Hungary and Russia in the years prior to 1914 encouraged some sections of opinion, including elements in the ruling circles, to contemplate war as a relief from such tensions and a possible means of avoiding social upheaval. For states such as Germany, Austria-Hungary and Russia, the empires which collapsed in 1917–18, this was perhaps the greatest of all the 'grand illusions' of pre-war Europe.

Making notes on 'The Origins of the First World War'

When reading this chapter, you need to be aware from the outset that you will be presented with a wide range of explanations of the causes of the war. Some of these interpretations are not compatible with others. Try to identify which they are. Fischer's views have had an enormous impact on modern scholarship, so you need to know what they are, whether you agree with them or not. You should also notice that when considering responsibility for the war, it can be helpful to distinguish between policies pursued before 1914 and during the July Crisis itself.

The notes you made from the previous chapter should contain useful information about the main events leading up to the war. The notes you take from this chapter should aim to provide you with a clear summary of each approach to the problem of war origins.

The following headings and sub-headings should assist you:
1. The debate on war origins
1.1. The polarities of the debate
2. Germany's responsibility
2.1. The views of the Fischer school. How convincing are they?
3. Responsibility of other powers
3.1. Austria-Hungary. How much importance would you give to their role?
3.2. Russia
3.3. France and Britain
4. The Balkans. How important a topic?
4.1. The Austro-Serb conflict
5. Alliances, anarchy, arms race
5.1. Changes in nature of alliances by 1914
5.2. International anarchy. Is this convincing?
5.3. Collapse of the concert. Does this seem significant?
5.4. Arms race
6. Capitalism, imperialism, nationalism
6.1. Anglo-German trade rivalry

6.2. Capitalist imperialism and the war $\left.\begin{array}{l}\\\\\end{array}\right\}$ Are these the same?
6.3. Imperial rivalries
7.   Conclusion.

Answering essay questions on 'The Origins of the First World War'

Although the range of questions asked on this topic is fairly wide, most of them focus on one of three issues: the alliance system and the balance of power; the Balkans; and responsibility for causing the war. You are much less likely to encounter a broad general question, examples of which are shown below after the main list.

Study the following questions, which have been arranged on the basis of the three main issues:

1 To what extent was the alliance system responsible for the outbreak of the First World War?
2 Why did the existence of the alliance system not prevent the outbreak of the war in 1914?
3 Discuss the view that 'War came in 1914 not because of the balance of power but because of its breakdown'.
4 Why and how did multinational problems in the Balkans and great power ambitions there develop into a European war in 1914?
5 'A Balkan war that got out of control'. Is this an adequate assessment of the events of 1914?
6 How far were Russian ambitions in the Balkans the main cause of the First World War?
7 How would you apportion responsibility for the outbreak of the First World War?
8 Should any one nation be seen as responsible for the outbreak of the First World War?
9 Which one of the European great powers was most responsible for the outbreak of war in 1914? Give reasons for your choice.
10 'The emphasis on German belligerence and war aims as an explanation of the outbreak of the First World War should not be allowed to obscure the obstinacy and aggression of other nations'. Consider this statement.
11 How far was German policy from 1898 responsible for the outbreak of war in 1914?
12 How far was the German government's decision to go to war in 1914 prompted by 'exaggerated fears of domestic and foreign threats to its security'?
13 Why did the Sarajevo murder but not the Agadir Crisis of 1911 lead to the outbreak of war?

14 Why did political rivalry in the Balkans, rather than economic rivalry in Africa, bring about the First World War?
15 'A European war about European issues'. Is this comment an adequate explanation of the origins of the war of 1914?
16 'Though war had long been expected by statesmen and peoples alike, its outbreak in 1914 came as a surprise and a shock'. Examine the truth of this statement.

You should be familiar now with the three different 'types' of question that are asked: 'the direct' question; the 'how far/to what extent' question; and the 'challenging statement' type of question. Taking questions 1 and 2 together, what differences would there be in your answers to them? For question 1, make two lists of three or four points (or paragraph headings) under two headings such as 'alliances' and 'other factors'. Arrange these points in order of importance and decide which list seems to be the stronger argument. Would you start the answer with a discussion of the role of the alliance system, since this is featured in the question? Question 2, a 'direct' question, clearly looks at the role of the alliance system from a different angle. Make a list of the five or six main causes of the war and consider why the alliance system did not act as a brake on them. What evidence would you use to back up each point of your case? Attempt an outline answer to question 3 on similar lines to question 1, by substituting 'balance of power' for 'alliance system'. If you are not satisfied with the result, what other approach might be appropriate for this 'challenging statement' question?

Look now at questions 4, 5 and 6. Use question 4, a 'direct' question, as a model which you could adapt to answer the other questions on the Balkans. What paragraph points would you make under the headings 'why' and 'how'? Under 'why' you would no doubt include pan-Slavism, Serbian nationalism and the south Slav problem. Take care not to let your response to 'how' become a lengthy recital of events from Sarajevo to the outbreak of war! Look again at your paragraph points under the 'why' heading. What additions and/ or subtractions would be needed for a framework for an answer to questions 5 and 6?

Questions 7, 8 and 9 are all 'direct' questions. Use question 7 as a model, and make a list of five or six paragraph points arranged in order of 'responsibility' (country by country would be appropriate). If Germany is top of the list, how many paragraphs would you devote to her – perhaps three? What re-thinking is necessary for the other two questions and how would you re-arrange your main points? Look closely now at questions 13 and 14. Both include the Balkans as one factor that caused the war, so that factor provides one of your two headings. The other heading could be why Agadir/imperialism did not cause war. Question 15, a 'challenging statement', lends itself to the 'how far' approach, with factors such as overseas ambitions/ imperialism as alternatives to European issues.

Question 16 is the 'odd man out' in its content. Possible headings would be 'true' and 'false'. You could usefully distinguish between crises and tension from 1905 to 1913 and the July Crisis itself.

If this discussion of so many questions is a little confusing you might find it useful to read it through again and review your responses.

Answering essay questions on *'International Relations 1870–1914'*

The main difference between questions in this section and the ones you have looked at in previous sections is that they cover a broader timespan and therefore require you to use information from more than one chapter.

Study the following questions:

1 Was the effect of colonial rivalries in the late nineteenth century to increase or diminish tension in Europe?

2 To what extent did colonial enterprise divert European nations from their other rivalries during the years 1870–1914?

3 'In 1870–71 Russia stood by as France was defeated; in 1894 the two countries signed an alliance.' What caused this change of attitude?

4 What benefits did France and Russia look for when making their alliance of 1894, and how far were their expectations realised during the next twenty years?

5 Is the term 'international anarchy' a satisfactory description of international relations between 1871 and 1914?

6 How justified were the other great powers in their suspicions concerning Russian designs in the Balkans in the half century before 1914?

7 Why did it prove impossible to solve the problems created by Balkan nationalism before 1914?

8 How and why had Europe become an armed camp by 1914?

9 Explain the fact that in 1914 the international alliances which had served the cause of peace since 1879 operated 'almost mechanically to convert a local conflict into a general war'.

These questions clearly cover a broad range of issues but five of them relate to topics you have already attempted questions on. Notice also that seven of them appear to be 'direct' questions – but questions 1 and 5 really require you to argue a case *for* and *against*.

Look at questions 1 and 2, which both explore the effect of colonial rivalries on international relations. It may seem odd that these rivalries could reduce tension in Europe, as the first question suggests.

However, if you prepare an essay plan for question 2, listing points under two appropriate headings, one set of points should provide some ideas for the 'reducing tension' part of question 1 – Russia diverted from the Near East to the Far East perhaps?

Questions 3 and 4 are both 'direct' questions on Franco-Russian relations, but with different timespans. Select one of these questions and prepare a list of five or six paragraph points. How much importance would you attach to 'fear of Germany' as a factor? Have you taken into account the 'anti-British' aspect of the Franco-Russian alliance from 1894 to 1904?

Question 5 is best treated as a 'how far' type of question. Be careful not to respond in a narrative way. Follow the usual approach for a 'direct' question when tackling question 7, and the 'how far' approach for question 6. Do you have several points of information common to both – such as Austria-Hungary's concern at slav nationalism, especially Serbia?

Questions 8 and 9 need the 'direct' question approach. What is the significance of the date in the last question? How much of your answers to these two questions would be devoted to a discussion of the effect of German policy on international relations in this period?

Finally, remember that you should try to avoid 'telling the story' in your essays. Identify the key points and try to discuss them. This is particularly important with the questions in this section which cover such a broad timespan.

Further Reading

There are hundreds of books on international relations and imperialism in the period 1870–1914. If your time for further reading is very limited, read chapters 5 to 8 of:
   F. R. Bridge and R. Bullen, *The Great Powers and the European States System, 1815–1914*, (Longman, 1980).

An alternative would be chapters 2, 5, 6 and 7 of:
   R. Langhorne, *The Collapse of the Concert of Europe*, (MacMillan Press, 1981).

They are both concise, possibly a little 'dense', but you should be able to enjoy them now that you have read an introductory work.

If you can spare more time, try some of these suggested titles. A useful brief, though rather old, biography of Bismarck which you would enjoy reading (chapters 4 to 6) is:
   W. N. Medlicott, *Bismarck and Modern Germany*, (The English Universities Press, 1965).

Imperialism is a fascinating but complex and controversial subject. You could dip your toes in the churning waters by reading pages 1 to 9 and 178 to 185 of:
   W. Baumgart, *Imperialism, The Idea and Reality of British and French Colonial Expansion, 1880–1914*, (Oxford University Press, 1982).

If you enjoy it, read chapters 2 and 3. Alternatively, if you want to read more on Africa, a short but fascinating book is:
   M. E. Chamberlain, *The Scramble for Africa*, (Longman, 1974).

On the causes of the 1914 war, an interesting and enjoyable book, despite its age is:
   L. C. F. Turner, *Origins of the First World War*, (Edward Arnold, 1970).

However, if you wish to be bang up to date, try at least the first two chapters of:
   J. Joll, *The Origins of the First World War*, (Longman, 1984).

For those with plenty of time and a taste for scholarly works, some quite different books which would repay reading are:
   P. Kennedy, *The Rise of the Anglo-German Antagonism, 1860–1914*, (George Allen & Unwin, 1982).

The most immediately relevant sections are Part 3 and Part 5. A more traditional treatment of German policy can be found in chapters 4, 7 and 9 of:
   G. A. Craig, *Germany, 1866–1945*, (Oxford University Press, 1978).

When the translation of Lothar Gall's new work on Bismarck becomes more widely available, it will delight many readers. Until then, and probably long after that, there are the chapters X to XIV of the monumental work:

A. J. P. Taylor, *The Struggle for Mastery in Europe, 1848–1918,* (Oxford University Press, 1954).

Sources on Rivalry and Accord: International Relations 1870–1914

Several relatively modern works contain useful and, at times, fascinating source material on this period.

1 **W. N. Medlicott and D. K. Coveney,** *Bismarck and Europe,* (Edward Arnold 1971)

On aspects of imperial rivalries, two very different collections are:
2 **C. J. Lowe,** *The Reluctant Imperialists, Vol. 2: The Documents,* (Routledge & Kegan Paul 1967)

3 **M. E. Chamberlain,** *The Scramble for Africa,* (Longman 1974)

More general coverage is given by:
4 **G. A. Kertesz,** *Documents in the Political History of the European Continent, 1815–1939,* (Oxford 1968)

On international issues from 1902 to 1914, there is useful material in parts 1 to 5 of:
5 **C. J. Lowe and M. L. Dockrill,** *The Mirage of Power, Vol. 3: The Documents,* (Routledge & Kegan Paul 1972)

On the July Crisis, there is:
6 **I. Geiss,** *July 1914, Select Documents,* (Batsford 1967)

For visual material, access to *Punch* and the *Illustrated London News* is desirable. *History Today* has some interesting pictures but the quality of the reproduction is sometimes poor.

Acknowledgements

The publishers would like to thank *Punch* magazine for their permission to reproduce all copyright illustrations.

The publishers would like to thank the following for their permission to reproduce copyright material:

Edward Arnold Limited for **W.N. Medlicott** and **D.K. Covenay**: *Bismarck and Europe*; Longman Group UK for **J.C.G. Rohl**: *From Bismarck to Hitler* and **D.K. Fieldhouse**: *The Theory of Capitalist Imperialism*; Century Hutchinson for **M. Balfour**: *The Kaiser and his Times*; Associated Book Publishers UK for **J.C. Lowe**: *The Reluctant Imperialists* (Routledge and Kegan Paul, 1967); Routledge and Kegan Paul for **C.C. Lowe** and **M.L. Dockrill**: *The Mirage of Power*, Vol 3; Oxford University Press for **G.A. Kertesz**: *Documents in the Political History of the European Continent* 1815–1939; Batsford for **I. Geiss**: *July 1914, Select Documents*; Allen & Unwin for **F. Kennedy**: *The Rise of the Anglo-German Antagonism*; David & Charles for **M. Hurst** (ed.): *Key Treaties for the Great Powers*, Vol. 2, 1871–1914; H.M.S.O. for **G.P. Gooch** and **H. Temperley** (eds.): *British Documents on the Origins of the War*, 1898–1914, Vol. 3

Index